SPIRITUAL WARFARE

IN MARRIAGE

Winning the Battle for a Good Marriage

BILL STONEBRAKER

Spiritual Warfare in Marriage
Winning the Battle for a Good Marriage

Copyright © 2017 by Bill Stonebraker

Published by Calvary Chapel of Honolulu, 98-1016 Komo Mai Drive, Aiea, Hawaii 96701.

First edition, 2000
Second edition, 2003
Third edition, 2005
Fourth edition 2009
Fifth edition 2010
Sixth edition 2017

ISBN 10: 1-931667-78-0

Printed in the United States of America
by Hagadone Printing Company

DEDICATION

To my loving wife Danita, who has remained steadfast and immovable, even when our lives were being sifted and tested to the breaking point. In seeking God's will above our own, He has truly given us beauty for ashes.

ACKNOWLEDGEMENT

I always tell young pastors, "Before you hire an assistant pastor, hire a good secretary. She will do the work of many assistants." My secretary Judi Marks is invaluable to the ministry. She has put in countless hours of time and effort toward this manuscript and innumerable other projects. My deepest thanks for her "quality control" and faithful dedication.

Finally, I want to thank my son, Bill Jr. ("Bud") – a gifted Bible teacher, a great supporter, and a persistent encourager – for insisting, "Dad, you need to write what you preach in a book."

CONTENTS

PREFACE

A few years ago, I felt very strongly about teaching a Saturday morning series entitled "Satan's Strategy in Marriage" for the married couples in our church. My conviction about this theme paid off. I discovered that the majority of the couples who attended were experiencing a great deal of spiritual warfare in their marriages and desperately needed tools to help them deal with their struggles.

My purpose in writing this book is to "get down into the trenches" with you in order to help you fight the battle for your marriage. The greatest asset my wife Danita and I have with which to instruct you is the fact that we survived gut-wrenching, teeth-gritting, nostril-flaring, vein-popping, skin-crawling, red-faced frustration in trying to work out our own marital difficulties – and by the grace of God, we have lived to tell about it.

I want to identify the areas of vulnerability where Satan attacks and give you helpful tips on how to beat the enemy in the battle for a good marriage. I pray that God might show you where the true struggle lies. It is not always obvious, nor is it necessarily in the domain of the visible, and it is hardly ever predictable.

One of my greatest blind spots was presuming that I knew the source of the problem. I made assumptions which were not based on fact, and that created a lot of tension. Proverbs 13:10a says, "Through presumption comes nothing but strife." The strategy of the enemy is to get us to believe lies while at the same time making us think we are right in our assumptions.

In this book, we will explore the many tactics used by the enemy to disrupt marital harmony, bringing division, and if possible, divorce. We will learn how to counterattack the Devil and defeat his ploys in the power of the Holy Spirit. Each chapter contains its own Study Guide to further strengthen your resolve for a godly marriage.

> *"We are more than conquerors through [Christ] who loved us."*
>
> –Romans 8:37 NRSV

CHAPTER ONE

KNOWING THE BATTLEFIELD

To be forewarned is to be forearmed.

Nadya and Peter

He was a handsome young composer. She was an heiress destined for wealth. To each, the other was beloved. Blossoming from their oneness came the most passionate music the world has ever known. She was Nadezhda (Nadya) von Meck. He was Peter Ilich Tchaikovsky.

Nadya was the wealthiest woman in Moscow, yet her vast, inherited fortune was little comfort in the wake of her husband's death. Devastated and heartbroken, she secluded herself in her magnificent mansion with an army of servants and attendants. The world was just beyond her doorstep, yet she was painfully alone. There was, however, a piano in the great mansion, and Nadya was a competent pianist. She played to soothe her wounds. Melodies became the expression of her melancholy; she played for herself the music she loved.

Meanwhile, in Moscow, there was a 36-year-old composer named Peter Ilich Tchaikovsky whose music was, unbeknownst to him, speaking eloquently to the heart of a lonely widow. It was as though he knew her secret longings and had spun them into an enchanted web of melodies and harmonies. He did not know that this woman, infatuated with Peter's music, was now taking a devoted interest in him personally, and that from his acquaintances, she was learning all about him: his temperament, longings, and desires. In the greatest of romantic traditions, Nadya had fallen in love – first with Peter's music, and then with Peter himself.

At last, she summoned up enough courage to introduce herself to him. Their relationship was polite in the beginning; "Honored Sir" and "Honored Madam" were their greetings. Nadya commissioned a number of Peter's musical compositions, becoming his patron, his mentor, and in time, his confidante and inspiration. Thus emerged one of the deepest and most intimate relationships in the history of music.

For fourteen years, they turned to each other for love in a lonely world, sharing each other's joys, and offering comfort in times of sorrow. For fourteen years, Peter's most sparkling and passionate music was written for Nadya, and for this, the world would forever owe her a debt of gratitude. To Peter, Nadya meant freedom itself; at times she was all there was between him and insanity.

Then one day they parted. It was Nadya who ended the relationship. No one knows exactly why, but neither survived very long without the other. Nadya's health deteriorated rapidly. Peter died, whispering her name. The secrets that did not die with them are preserved in their correspondence. In fact, it contains all that we know about them and all that they knew about each other. For Peter and Nadya, this intense romance in music – the love of a lonely heiress for a handsome young composer and his love for her – was oneness at a distance. Nadya and Peter, for fear of shattering the beautiful illusion, confined their love to letters for fourteen years. Never once did they meet.[1]

The Real World

Like Nadya and Peter, my wife Danita and I could also have had a model marriage – if we had a *letters-only* relationships – but in the real world, it is simply not that way. If nuptials were confined solely to paper and ink, there would be no difficulties. Each partner would always be on his or her best behavior, never grumpy or rude to each other. However, reality is more like the husband's quip when asked, "When you get up in the morning, do you wake up grumpy?" To which he replied, "No, I just let her sleep!"

The challenge in marriage is not to let little things divide you. Solomon pictures these squabbles as foxes in the vineyard. *"Catch the foxes for us, the little foxes that are ruining the vineyards"* (Song of Solomon 2:15). This is true for any couple living together for a lifetime.

When I hear people say, "We have never had an argument in all the years we've been married," I think to myself: *Do you ever see each other? Do you ever talk to each other? Are you both still breathing?* That is certainly not the way it has been for Danita and me. Both of us are charter members of "Club Disagreement." We have had to learn to come to terms with each other's strong and sometimes unyielding personalities and opinions.

The Apostle Paul, who had clear insight into human nature, said of marriage: *"Such will have trouble in this life … [the] one who is married is concerned about the things of the world, how he may please his wife, and his interests are divided. [And the woman] … who is married is concerned about the things of the world, how she may please her husband"* (1 Corinthians 7:28, 33-34).

Even in healthy marriages, it is common to experience both seasons of tranquility and seasons of turmoil. How do you deal with trouble when it comes? What steps can you take so that your marriage is not divided? The experts tell us that one out of every two marriages ends in divorce.[2] That is like having a flip-of-a-coin chance of marital success. Statistics are not in your favor, but "if Christ is for you, who can be against you?" (Romans 8:31).

The Enemy's Plot

The thief comes only to steal, and kill, and destroy; I came that they may have life, and have it abundantly.

– John 10:10

The Devil hates your marriage and plans to do everything in his power to destroy it. When a marriage breaks up, I often hear excuses such as: "We've grown apart, we're no longer compatible," or "I fell out of love with my spouse and into love with someone else," or "I have grown out of the relationship," or "I have changed directions in my life." The list goes on. One great failure in marriage is not recognizing the unseen spiritual forces at work to undo *"what God has joined together"* (Matthew 19:6 NKJV).

Take a moment...

Are you looking for an "acceptable excuse" to get out of your marriage? Take stock of any "cop-outs" you have been entertaining and take a moment right now to repent, reaffirming your commitment to God and your mate.

A fierce battle rages between the prince of the power of the air, Satan, and Jesus Christ, the Lord of light and life. Jesus died on the cross and rose from the dead to save us.

When we believe in Him, we are born again by His Spirit. Once a person is born again, he is placed into the Body of Christ, the Church. The attack of Satan is therefore not only against marriage, but also against the Church to which the married couple belongs.

Marriage is a microcosm of Christ and the Church. God ordained only two institutions: marriage and the Church. They are likened to each other in Ephesians 5:31-32: *"For this reason a man shall leave his father and mother and shall be joined to his wife, and the two shall become one flesh. This mystery is great; but I am speaking with reference to Christ and the church."* Since the Bible says that "the gates of hell shall not prevail against [the church]" (see Matthew 16:18), the Devil goes after the weakest link in the chain of the Church – fragile marriages.

Get ready for conflict. *To be forewarned is to be forearmed.* We must know our enemy. Behind marital conflict lurks a fiendish foe, who takes the most trivial disagreements and blows them out of proportion, making it seem impossible to live with each other. The Devil delights in chaos, confusion, and conflict.

I can recall one such situation in my own marriage. The final scene – as I imagined it – showed Danita and me standing in divorce court. The judge inquired, "Why are you here?" and we answered, "Pork chop bones, your Honor." Then we proceeded to tell the real-life story of *The Pork Chop Bone Caper* – a tale of how the enemy took the trivial and turned it into the traumatic.

This is what actually happened:

We were working around the house and yard, and Danita happened to be mowing the lawn. While she was outside, I passed through the kitchen and noticed some pork chop bones in a bowl on the counter. *How nice, I thought to myself, All of these months, my wife has been collecting leftover pork chop bones and freezing them for the dogs.* So I proceeded to pour the dry dog food into their bowls, dumped in the pork chop bones, and added water. As I came out the door to the backyard with the bowls in hand, Danita saw the bones and hollered, "What are you doing? Those are the pork chop bones I was saving to put in the spaghetti sauce for dinner tonight!" I laughed, but she stormed back to the lawn mower.

It was an honest mistake and funny to me, but she thought it was deadly serious. The problem? First, I did not ask, "What are these bones for, Dear?" before I put them into the dogs' dishes. Second, she was doing the mowing, and I was not! I thought she liked to cut the grass with our new power mower, but in reality she was just disappointed that I had put it off for another day. Third, that stash of bones in the freezer was like a bank account to her: it took awhile, but she had finally saved enough bones for the spaghetti sauce. My final mistake was following her out to the lawn mower, which was now idling at full throttle. Unable to hold back my amusement over the situation, with a snicker I asked, "Do you want me to rinse off the bones?" She glared back, "You figure it out."

I went back into the house and for a half-second considered washing them off, but decided against it. Instead, I let the dogs feast on what should have been a key ingredient in the spaghetti sauce that night.

Before long we talked about what had happened, but I could not help smiling and letting out an occasional chuckle, even as Danita was expressing her hurt feelings over my thoughtless actions. Each smirk on my part created greater frustration on hers.

I said, "Hun, just wait until a little time passes. We will both look back on this situation and laugh."

But her mood worsened. Finally, I started getting as irritated as she was and it escalated into a war zone. *Little foxes can ruin the vineyard.* Can you imagine getting a divorce over pork chop bones? I think situations like this are what the courts call "irreconcilable differences."

Take a moment...

In addition to *chasing the foxes*, marriage partners should also *spare the scapegoats.* In what ways have you made your spouse a scapegoat for your marital failures?

Psychological counselors often state the obvious in explaining why strife exists in a relationship. It could be neglect, a breakdown in communication, or just irresponsibility. William Glasser, the author of *Reality Therapy*, observes that a person who is unable to fulfill his essential needs – especially for love and self-worth – denies the reality of the world around him and acts irresponsibly. In order to make him face a truth which he has spent a lifetime trying to avoid, he is made to be responsible for his behavior.[3]

The Bible goes beyond the obvious and looks to the root cause of much marital discord and break ups – Satan's strategy to steal, kill, and destroy. Couples who survive intense marital disharmony can look back in hindsight and see how the Devil was able to distort reality, stir up strife, and cause confusion. He takes the *minuscule* and makes it *monumental.*

When the Serpent engaged Eve in conversation in Genesis 3, she became the unwitting victim of distorted reality: "God knows that in the day you eat from the tree of knowledge of good and evil your eyes will be opened, and you will be like God, knowing good and evil" (see v. 5). Satan made it appear that God was holding out on Eve, keeping her from some hidden pleasure – a secret treasure she could only obtain by violating her conscience and disobeying God. Satan convinced Eve that the end justified the means, that the gratification she would gain by eating would outweigh any penalty for breaking God's command not to eat. She was *dead wrong*. What God had meant for good, the Devil turned around and made appear evil. He distorted reality.

When they ate the fruit, an instant separation took place – death and division followed on its heels. A relationship that was once harmonious, loving, and good, turned hostile, accusatory, and bitter. When God confronted the couple, asking, "Have you eaten from the tree of which I commanded you not to eat?" Adam said, "It is the woman You gave me. She made me eat!" Eve started out as Adam's *helpmate*, but soon became his *scapegoat,* as strife entered the Garden of Eden.

Confusion seeps into a relationship when God's Word is ignored and one or both partners decide to "do their own thing." After Eve sinned, Adam followed suit and ate the forbidden fruit. It has been suggested that he did so out of love for Eve and a sense of responsibility for not protecting her in time of temptation. Unfortunately, it separated him from fellowship with God. *"How can two walk together unless they are agreed?"* (Amos 3:3 NKJV). *"God is not a God of confusion"* (1 Corinthians 14:33). Confusion comes into a relationship when we give in to temptation and compromise the Word of God.

My wife Danita and I have been married for over four decades, but there was a time when we both wanted out of our marriage. Today we love each other more than ever and would not trade what God has done in our lives for anything. During those difficult years, I had it in my mind that she was the problem, and to her I was the problem. After each battle, when the dust had settled and we were found among the marital survivors, we saw how the Devil had obscured our true feelings of love for each other and made fleeting issues – which we now cannot even remember – seem insurmountable. Today, we are experientially wise to the schemes of the Devil. We see how Satan takes insignificant problems and blows them out of proportion, causing us to believe they are grounds for divorce.

You may be experiencing extreme pressure in your relationship with your spouse: things seem intolerable and you are ready to throw in the towel and quit. But wait a minute! Have you considered the real source of the problem? It goes beyond the physical realm. Until we recognize the real battlefield and understand who our true enemy (the Devil) is, we will never be able to deal with the actual issues that divide us, or be able to free ourselves from Satan's devices.

The Real Battle

Statistics prove that a higher percentage of second marriages end in divorce than first marriages.[4] You can imagine the Devil behind the scenes, whispering lies to troubled couples: "The grass will be greener the next time around. Go ahead, dump the moron, and move on."

All couples go through difficult times and have to make adjustments in order to achieve marital harmony. Satan does his best to divert our attention away from the root of the problem by sending a subterfuge, such as a co-worker of the opposite sex in whom one partner innocently begins to confide. This is a bad idea under any circumstance. That sympathetic ear is easily used by the enemy as bait to catch his prey – YOU. The person may be so understanding and compassionate that finally you think: *Here is someone who is willing to take the time and really listen to my feelings.* That leads inevitably to comparison: *I wish my spouse were as understanding and kind as this person is.*

Suddenly, the battlefield changes. Marital adjustment is no longer the problem. Now the difficulty is emotional entanglement with this sympathetic someone who is not your mate. Your mind mulls over leaving your mate for this exciting new relationship. You have visions of "living happily ever after" with this person whom you think cares for you so deeply and understands you so completely.

In reality, Satan has gone fishing and you have been caught! According to statistics, those who divorce once are more likely to divorce again. In fact, sixty percent of second marriages end in divorce.[5] Why? Because reality shatters the enemy's cleverly created fantasy. As you settle down once again into the daily routine of dirty dishes, demands at the office, and paying the bills, you find that this new relationship, which seemed so promising, is actually not much different from the one you abandoned. You are still dealing with self-centered human nature and relationship problems. The only difference is the person you wake up next to in the morning.

This is Satan's recruiting process. He paints a tantalizing illusion of the ideal – how perfect life would be if you were with this person who is not your spouse. Somehow, you buy into the lie. The deception says that it is okay to leave all that you know to be true about marriage and what is right in God's eyes to chase after this unrealistic fantasy, rooted in compromise and deception.

Take a moment...

Satan goes fishing for marriages to destroy.

Is he dangling any bait in front of you right now?

What will you do to cut the line?

A letter to Ann Landers sums up the emotional aftermath of deciding to bail out on a spouse and pursue the illusion of love. The person writes:

Dear Ann,

I would like to share my story because I know a lot of people think of their lives the way I thought of mine.

Sometimes you feel lonely and unloved in a marriage, even after 23 years. You feel as if there has got to be more to life, so you set out to find someone who can make you blissfully happy.

You believe that you have found that someone and decide he is exactly what you want. So you pack up and say goodbye to that 23-year marriage and all the friends you made when you were part of a couple. You give your children the option of coming with you or staying with their father.

You live the glorious life for a few years and then a light bulb goes on in your head. You realize that you have exactly the life that you had before – the only difference is that you've lost your friends, your children's respect and the best friend you loved and shared everything with for 23 years. And you miss him. You realize that love does not just happen; it must be nurtured through the years. You cannot undo what has been done, so you settle for a lonely and loveless life with emptiness in your heart.

Ann, please print my letter so others will not give up something that is truly precious and let them know that they won't know how precious it is until they have thrown it away.

– Heavy-Hearted In Philly[6]

What a heartbreaking story! Those who have not made this mistake – or who do not want to make it again – need to realize that *to be forewarned is to be forearmed*. Know the battlefield. The Devil is the master of illusion. He makes things appear to be what they are not, so he can bring pain and misery into a person's life.

The following humorous story illustrates how the Devil cleverly disguises reality. Of course, the results of Satan's schemes are not funny at all, but the story makes a chilling point:

A very successful litigating attorney died suddenly of a heart attack. His soul arrived in Heaven and was met by Gabriel who told him, "Before you get too comfortable up here, we have a slight problem. We have never had a lawyer make it this far and so we are not quite sure what to do with you."

The man replied, "Just let me come in."

"I can't," Gabriel answered. "I've got orders to let you spend a day in Heaven and a day in hell, and then you can choose where you want to spend eternity."

The man said, "But I think I'd like to be up here."

"Sorry," Gabe told him, "rules are rules." And with that the lawyer was put on an elevator and went down ... down ... down ... to hell.

The doors opened and he found himself stepping onto the manicured putting green of a beautiful golf course. There stood a magnificent country club with all his friends and fellow attorneys dressed in fine clothes. They ran up to the new candidate and hugged him, patting him on the back and talking about old times.

The attorney and his friends played a couple rounds of golf and that evening dined on steak and lobster. The Devil himself served as master of ceremonies. He was warm and cordial and personally acknowledged the new guest. They laughed and danced the night away and suddenly it was time to leave. They all said their tearful goodbyes, wishing the man could stay.

He got on the elevator and it went up ... up ... up ... opening this time in Heaven. Gabriel met him with a joyful greeting: "Now it's time for you to spend a day in Heaven."

The attorney had a great time in Heaven, as well, and finally the question was put to him: "You have spent a day in Heaven and a day in hell, which do you choose for your eternal home?"

The lawyer paused for a moment and then said, "You know, I have always heard how great Heaven is – and don't get me wrong – it is everything they said it was supposed to be. But I have also heard how horrible hell is, and I find it to be just the opposite. All my friends were there and I really had a great time. I never thought I would say this, but I think I would rather go to hell."

Puzzled, Gabriel looked at the man and said, "Are you sure? Once you get back on the elevator, it is a done deal. This time it will only go one way."

The lawyer said, "I am sure."

He was put back on the elevator, which went down ... down ... down ... back to hell. This time when the doors opened, he stepped out and found himself in a desolate wasteland covered with refuse and filth. He could hear horrible wailing in the background and began gagging from the suffocating heat. He saw his friends once again, but this time they were despondent, dressed in dirty rags, picking up garbage and putting it into sacks.

The Devil greeted the man, who exclaimed, "Yesterday when I was here it was so beautiful: the golf course, the country club, my friends were so happy and dressed so well. We ate steak and lobster, and danced and laughed the night away. What happened? This is a wasteland! All my friends look so miserable!"

The Devil sneered at the lawyer and said with disdain, "Yesterday I was recruiting – today you are on staff."

You will always be disappointed when you leave the Lord and all that you know to be true about His Word and sovereign plan for your life to follow the enemy and his lies. Satan seeks to convince you that it would be better to leave the person you married and run off with this wonderful new person who will make you marvelously happy.

Today there is a new mistress and a new Casanova to contend with, one who comes right into the home in pursuit of the lonely, the bored, and the flirtatious. It is called *Internet Infidelity*. "Online affairs have become so commonplace and typical, I can almost write the script," said relationship's expert and author Peggy Vaughn. "In fact, people have been known to risk it all by leaving their partner before they meet the new person in the flesh."[7]

Washington D.C. divorce attorney Sanford Ain remarked, "Often, Internet affairs precipitate divorce. Married couples harmed by a partner's meandering seldom stay together."[8]

Psychologist Debbie Layton-Tholl of Boca Raton, Florida, said, "The Internet is the second-largest way of meeting people and having affairs."[9] She went on to add the following ...

> When people talk to me about their experience on the Internet and tell me, "I'm in love, he's my soul mate," it's incredible. They are talking about passion that I can only imagine having in an intimate contact with somebody, and they are having this in electronic communications never having seen or touched this individual.
>
> These are mature adults, married people with kids, with responsible jobs, and they are changing their lives because of what starts out as a fantasy.
>
> You become obsessive and preoccupied and the arousal continues to increase because that is the nature of fantasy. People are falling head over heels passionately. It's out there.[10]

Another psychologist who studied this phenomenon was Dr. Shirley Glass, author of the book *Not "Just Friends"*. Glass wrote:

> Fantasy is what makes these Internet affairs unique. People only reveal a part of themselves on the Internet, which leads to a romantic image based on illusion, she says. Using fantasy as a catalyst ... the fling can be very intense from the beginning.

You don't have to have physical contact to have an affair. ... The thing it has in common is the secrecy, the emotional intimacy and the sexual chemistry.[11]

Take a moment...

Are you willing to share your internet history with your spouse? Are you hiding any online relationships from your mate? How can you be more accountable to one another regarding time spent online?

The Devil is recruiting and if you fall for it, you will soon discover, as did the person who wrote to Ann Landers, that the second state is worse than the first. Yet, there is tremendous hope for those who are contemplating leaving and even for those who may have already left. No matter what has taken place in your life up to this point, God has a plan for you right now. No one has ever made a mistake so big that God cannot fix it.

Romans 8:28 says: *"And we know that God causes all things to work together for good to those who love God, to those who are called according to His purpose."* If you will commit your ways to the Lord, He will take even the worst situation and make something good from it. He will take wasted years, ruined opportunities, and wrong decisions and turn them around. He is forever a God of redemption. Joel 2:25 says that He will *"restore the years that the canker-worm and locust have eaten."* In other words, when we come to Him for help, He will overrule our misspent years and ruined lives, bringing worth and value.

God has done this for countless couples and can do it for you and your mate. My prayer is that God will show you that His power and grace are not limited to the stories of other people, but are available for your life today. The redeeming love of God always brings *"beauty for ashes, the oil of joy for mourning, the garment of praise for the spirit of heaviness"* (Isaiah 61:3 NKJV). May it be so in your life as you continue to read.

LET'S DISCUSS
KNOWING THE BATTLEFIELD...

1. Have you ever thought of marriage as a battlefield? Who is the battle really between? Are husbands and wives meant to be on opposing sides or on the same side?

2. What can a person do to maintain a proper perspective of the real enemy in his or her marriage?

3. Some people think that the state of their marriage doesn't affect anyone else. Is that really true? Let's consider the battle's aftermath.

    a. Think about a marriage you know that has ended, and ask yourself:

    How did it affect their immediate family?

    How did it affect their extended families?

    How did it affect their friends?

    How did it affect their church life (if they were believers)?

    b. Does it affect the Church as a whole when one Christian marriage is destroyed?

    Explain your answer.

4. As you think about Bill and Danita's "Pork Chop Bone Caper" story:

    a. What do you think Bill did wrong?

    b. What do you think Danita did wrong?

    c. What could they have done differently in order to avoid the conflict?

LET'S APPLY WHAT WE'VE LEARNED...

1. We have examined some of the reasons people give as excuses for breaking their marriage vows. Fill in the columns below.

Reasons I Should Not Keep My Vows	Reasons I Should Keep My Vows

   a. Now ask yourself, who is the real author of each column?

   b. Which column would the devil want you to tear up and throw away?

   c. Which column would the Lord want you to tear up and throw away? Will you do it?

2. We saw how the enemy often seeks to blow insignificant problems out of proportion, turning the trivial into the traumatic.

   Think of a "pork chop bone" fiasco-type event from your own marriage. Now that you understand the real nature of marital battles, consider the following questions:

a. What could you have done differently?

b. How did you misread the situation? What was the real issue? What affected your perspective?

3. The Bible tells us that husbands and wives should be concerned with pleasing their mates. Think about what pleases your husband or wife. Are you doing anything with that knowledge?

4. Have you ever honestly given Christ his rightful place as Head of your marriage and home?

    a. If you have, can you give some examples that show it?

    b. If you haven't made that commitment as a couple, are you willing to come together and make it now?

CHAPTER TWO

DEFEATING THE PAST

You write bitter accusations against me and bring up all the sins of my youth.

— Job 13:26 NLT

The name Job has become synonymous with trials and tribulations. Here was a man who seemed to have it all — family, friends, health, and wealth — then he lost it practically overnight. His wife was not much help either. She counseled Job to *"curse God and die"* (Job 2:9).

When Job spoke the words quoted above from Job 13:26, he was deeply troubled and hurting. From the depths of his misery, he reasoned that God was punishing him for his misspent youth. In reality, God was Job's biggest fan. He bragged about him in Heaven, but Satan challenged God's boast, saying, "Job is a mercenary. He serves You because of what You've given him. Take it all away and he'll curse You to Your face. You have put a hedge around him and I can't get to him." So for a time, God allowed Satan access to Job's life, causing the ensuing turmoil.

People often blame God for the chaos the Devil causes. The Bible tells us about one occasion when Jesus told the disciples to cross over to the other side of the Sea of Galilee without Him. A storm arose and they found themselves in distress, until Jesus came and calmed the storm. Who caused the storm? Could it have been Satan seeking to discourage the disciples from obeying Jesus' command? The Devil will do whatever he can to discourage you from obeying God.

Satan has a way of taking our past sins and bringing them into our present situation in order to hinder the work God wants to do in our lives.

Take a moment...

Have you allowed the enemy to exploit a shaky beginning to your marriage? Is that casting doubt on your relationship? Are you using it to justify bailing out on your marriage?

Isaiah 43:18 says, *"Do not call to mind the former things, or ponder things of the past."* This is exactly what the Devil does. He takes the mistakes of the past and throws them in your face, trying to ruin the good work God is seeking to do presently. The use of unresolved conflict between husbands and wives is his specialty. He tries to keep past resentment fresh in your mind, knowing it will help shape your current opinion of your mate. What is the effect? Those "former things" distort your perception of what you are dealing with today. It is difficult enough to resolve conflict in the present without bringing in baggage from the past. Spend whatever time it takes to settle past issues, then leave them in the past – forgiven, forgotten, and resolved.

A person once revealed to me that their partner had been unfaithful. The affair had long since ended and there had been radical repentance and contrition. Now supposedly it was all in the past – forgiven and forgotten. Since that time, however, it became normal for this couple to end every disagreement whether big or small in a standoff, with neither person willing to give ground. The bickering and unwillingness to yield to the other's point of view seemed nonsensical until they realized that each saw the other through the lens of unresolved conflict. Past sins repented of were not really forgiven and forgotten; at every turn the offended party was looking for groveling, mortification, and signs of contrition from the one who had committed the sin in order to prove just how sorry they really were. In response, the once-guilty, now-repentant party held their ground, fighting for dignity, identity, and the need to feel forgiven. *Holding on to the past was destroying what God had for them in the present.*

We must see our mate's sins as God sees them: forgiven and forgotten. In both the Old and New Testaments God says He will not *remember* our sins; literally, He "will not keep a record of them." Jeremiah 31:34 says, *"For I will forgive their iniquity, and their sin I will remember no more."* This also carries the idea of not throwing our sins back in our faces to remind us just how bad we are. Hebrews 10:17 adds, *"And their sins and their lawless deeds I will remember no more."*

See your mate the way God sees them. That will give them the freedom to grow into the husband or wife God intends them to be. You might say that God looks at us through rose-colored glasses. Of course, in His case, they are bloodstained glasses. God sees us forgiven in Christ; we need to see our mates the same way.

Part One: Less-Than-Ideal Beginnings

Just as He chose us in Him before the foundation of the world, that we would be holy and blameless before Him in love.

– Ephesians 1:4

God knew us before we knew Him. His hand was upon our lives even before we were saved. We were in His mind before the foundation of the world, and His providence has been ruling in our lives; nothing has been able to stop it. Satan, however, sends us a mixed message about marriage. He tries to get us to doubt our present condition based on past circumstances. Couples who were married under less-than-ideal conditions start listening to his whispers: "The reason you are having so much trouble in your marriage is because God was not guiding you when you got married." Satan tells us, "Your relationship was not really the sovereign plan of God. It was accidental. It is a product of the flesh – thus your marriage is not really of God."

Once Satan has succeeded in causing a couple to question God's providence and sovereignty over their lives and their marriage, he will continue to whisper his lies in their ears, saying, "God does not want you in an unhappy relationship. Get out of this marriage and find God's best for you." When they listen to the lies of the enemy, they begin to believe that they need to get out of their marriage and start all over again – this time with the "perfect mate" God has chosen for them. If Satan can convince them that their marriage is of their own doing and not of God's providence, they will often look for a way out when times get tough.

The Bible tells us God is sovereign over all situations. *"Before I formed you in the womb I knew you, and before you were born I consecrated you"* (Jeremiah 1:5). However carnal and sordid your past may have been, the sovereign hand of God has been with you since before you were born. Do not let the enemy distort this truth.

The Past Providence of God over David and Bathsheba's Lives

Some well-known heroes of the faith also had shaky and sordid beginnings, yet God blessed and used them. Second

Samuel 11 tells a scandalous story of David and Bathsheba, yet we see how the providence of God overruled their sinful decisions and brought good out of their bad choices.

"At the time when kings go out to battle ... David stayed at Jerusalem" (v. 1). Idle hands are the Devil's workshop, or so the saying goes. When David should have been out fighting, he was flirting. Unable to sleep one night, he walked along his rooftop and saw a beautiful woman bathing. High rank demands high responsibility, so, as king of Israel, David should have turned away, gone back to bed, put a pillow over his head, and prayed: "Lord, I am lusting. Please help me! I cannot get these images out of my mind. Help me to resist!"

At this point, maybe he should have called for Nathan the prophet to come with the Torah to read him a bedtime story. Instead, David inquired about the woman. "She is Bathsheba," he was told, "the wife of Uriah." This Uriah was a soldier in David's army, currently in battle fighting for the honor of Israel, as David should have been.

King David commanded that Bathsheba be brought to him. The text tells us *"he lay with her"* and she became pregnant. Then he sought to cover his sin by calling her husband home from the front lines, using the pretense that Uriah was to deliver a combat report. David assumed that while Uriah was home, he would sleep with his wife. Then everyone would presume that Uriah was the baby's father. However, after giving the king his report, Uriah did not go home. Instead, he slept with the servants at the door of the house of David.

"Why didn't you go home to be with your wife?" David asked the next morning. Uriah replied, "The Ark of the Covenant and the army of Israel are at battle. How could I take pleasure with my wife?" The *ignominy* of David was only magnified by the *integrity* of Uriah.

The next night David got Uriah drunk. Surely he would become amorous and lie with his wife. But Uriah stuck to his principles, once again sleeping on the porch with David's servants. Now David sank even deeper into depravity, sending a sealed message to his commander Joab by Uriah's own hand, saying, "Go into battle, close to the enemy's walls. Put Uriah on the front line. Then pull back from him that he might die!"

When word came back to David that the deed was done, Bathsheba went into mourning; not long after, she and David were married. For two years, David lived under the cloud of his transgressions. Finally, Nathan the prophet confronted him with his sin, using this allegory:

> *There were two men in one city, the one rich and the other poor. The rich man had a great many flocks and herds. But the poor man had nothing except one little ewe lamb which he bought and nourished; and it grew up together with him and his children. It would eat of his bread and drink of his cup and lie in his bosom, and was like a daughter to him. Now a traveler came to the rich man, and he was unwilling to take from his own flock or his own herd, to prepare for the wayfarer who had come to him; rather he took the poor man's ewe lamb and prepared it for the man who had come to him.*
>
> – 2 Samuel 12:1-4

David's righteous indignation rose up within him, and he demanded the rich man pay back four times what he had taken, exclaiming, "He deserves to die!" Nathan looked at him and declared, "David, you are the man! You stole the wife of Uriah. You could have had any woman in your kingdom, yet you took the wife of another man. You are the guilty one."

David repented and cried out, "I have sinned against the Lord!" Nathan told him, "The Lord also has taken away your sin, and you shall not die." *(It is important to recognize that in the case of true repentance, forgiveness is instantaneous.)* But Nathan went on to say that although David would not die, the child would. David fasted and prayed, but the baby still died. Afterward David reflected, "The child will not come back to me, but I will go to be with the child" (see 2 Samuel 12:23).

After that infamous beginning, David and Bathsheba had another son named Solomon, of whom Nathan the prophet said, "For the Lord's sake his name shall be Jedidiah, which is translated 'beloved of the Lord' " (see 2 Samuel 12:12). So even a wretched beginning, when put into the hands of God, can have a blessed ending. Solomon succeeded his father David as king of Israel and is found in the genealogy of Jesus Christ.

Like David and Bathsheba, you may have started out all wrong, but God can make things right again if you will simply yield your life to Him. *"And we know that God causes all things to work together for good to those who love God, to those who are called according to His purpose"* (Romans 8:28).

Surely there were times when David and Bathsheba looked at each other across the breakfast table and thought, "I don't like you!" Maybe David said, "Why were you bathing openly on the rooftop, anyway? What kind of a woman would do a thing like that? Where was your modesty?" Bathsheba, at this point, might have returned his barb with, "Well, what kind of guy snoops around on rooftops like a *Peeping Thomas*? You knew I was married, and you still called for me. You are just as guilty!" They must have had a lot of obstacles to overcome; yet ultimately, God blessed their relationship.

Danita and I can speak from experience to couples who have started out wrong and now want to do what is right in the eyes of God. We met when she was thirteen and I was seventeen. We were married three years later under less-than-ideal circumstances, and for the next seven years, we did everything imaginable to destroy each other and our relationship. Then I received Christ. About a year later, Danita accepted the Lord.

Even though we both had become Christians – reading our Bibles, going to church, and having Bible studies in our home – it still took many years for the Lord to untangle the mess that we had made of our lives. There were times when I thought the relationship was definitely not the will of God because we had such a poor beginning and were experiencing so much strife. Yet, as we made it through each trial, we were able to look back and clearly see the hand of God upon our lives all the way.

God is now able to use our troubled past to minister to other couples going through similar struggles. I have great faith for problem marriages. If the couple will determine not to give up, but instead to ride out the marital storms, and to trust God in their relationship, He will abundantly bless them.

Unwilling to Forgive

The sorrow that is according to the will of God produces a repentance without regret, leading to salvation; but the sorrow of the world produces death.

– 2 Corinthians 7:10

Convincing couples that God was not involved in the formation of their relationship – that instead it was all their carnal doing – is one of Satan's favorite strategies for destroying a marriage. Another of his schemes is to bring up past sins in order to ruin the work God is doing in the present. There is a big difference between past sins that have been repented of and those for which no repentance has been made.

When a partner sins grievously and does not show evidence of true contrition, a definite problem arises. Are they sorry because they got caught and now feel uncomfortable? Is theirs a worldly sorrow? Or is it a life-changing, godly sorrow, where the repentance is as notorious as the sin?

We read earlier in Job 13:26 how Job reasoned, *"You write bitter accusations against me and bring up all the sins of my youth"* (NLT).

The Devil can create dissension in the home when one partner continues to bring an accusation against the other over a sin for which they have truly repented. The Bible tells us in Psalm 25:7, *"Do not remember the sins of my youth or my transgressions; according to Your lovingkindness remember me, for Your goodness' sake, O LORD."*

If the Lord does not hold our sins against us or bring them to remembrance anymore, we should not hold our mate's past sins against them either. To remember the sins of your spouse – whether they were committed last week, last year, or twenty years ago – and then to use them as a wrecking ball, will destroy your marriage. You will be at a stalemate, a state of arrested marital growth, never being able to move forward into the blessings that God has for your marriage.

Take a moment...

On the basis of your **present** willingness to forgive your mate's past sins, would your marriage be able to move forward? If there are any obstacles, are you now willing to lay them at the foot of the cross?

Beauty and the Beast

In 1 Samuel 25, we read about a beautiful woman who had a horrible husband. It is an Old Testament version of *Beauty and the Beast*. Abigail is the beauty and her husband Nabal is the beast. He stays that way throughout the story though; no happy ending for this beast.

David and his men were on the run from Saul when they came to a place called Maon. Nabal, a wealthy resident of the area, had left his sheep with his servants and had gone to Carmel to do business. While he was away, David and his men camped around Nabal's flocks to protect them from marauding bands of thieves in the area. Later, in return for this favor, David sent messengers to tell Nabal of this good deed and ask him to return the favor by supplying some provisions for his men, which was a customary hospitality of the day. Nabal insulted David's integrity by rudely replying: "Who is David but a runaway slave? He's a rebel in the kingdom, and I'll have nothing to do with him." Enraged, David girded on his sword and declared: "Surely in vain I have guarded this man's goods ... he has returned me evil for good. He's a dead man!"

Word of David's anger got back to Abigail, Nabal's wife. We don't know much about this woman, except that "she was beautiful and intelligent." Abigail immediately began preparing provisions, sending servants ahead to meet

David and to intercede on her behalf. "Excuse us, David, the woman of the house is on her way with the provisions you asked for. Could you kindly put your sword away for a minute and listen to what she has to say?" They told David it was a known fact in those parts that Nabal was hardheaded and had a reputation for being "worthless." His servants knew it, and his wife knew it. Nabal had a flawed character.

David encountered Abigail, who bowed down before him saying, "Have mercy on us and don't take the Lord's revenge into your own hands." Here was a spiritual woman exhorting the future king of Israel not to act on his own behalf, but to trust God to do what needed to be done. She told David:

Please do not let my lord pay attention to this worthless man, Nabal, for as his name is, so is he. Nabal is his name and folly is with him; but I your maidservant did not see the young men of my lord whom you sent.

– 1 Samuel 25:25

In essence, Abigail was saying, "Because my husband is acting like a fool, that is no reason for you to do the same. Nabal is his name, and folly is his game!" As she was speaking, David came to his senses and praised her perception, calling her blessed. David received the provisions and sent her away in peace.

When Abigail returned home, she looked for an appropriate time to tell her husband what she had done: namely, having saved Nabal's stubborn life along with his household. Nabal was throwing a huge party and had gotten drunk, so Abigail waited until he was sober to tell him. Perhaps she had learned that alcohol and abuse flow from the same bottle.

In the morning, *"when the wine went out of him,"* she

broke the news to Nabal, telling him why he and the others were not now dead. Upon hearing her words, the heart of Nabal *"died within him"* so that it became as a stone. He was such a hardhearted man that when his wife violated his will, even for the betterment of his own family, his ego could not handle it. His pride refused to accept it. Instead of softening his heart, he became hardened and *"ten days later he died."*

Take a moment...

Unforgiveness cost Nabal his life.

What has it cost you?

The Nabal in All of Us

Harboring unforgiveness not only destroys a marriage, but it also destroys the person who is unwilling to forgive. Once sins have been repented of, they need to be forgotten. If we continue to brood over past sins of which others have repented, we will not be able to move forward with what God has for us in the future.

Reading this story of Abigail and Nabal causes us to conclude that she was right and he was wrong. Most men would not like to think that they treat their wives the way Nabal treated Abigail (and hopefully they do not), yet I believe there is a *Nabal-side* to all of us. If we as men do not check our attitudes, we may find ourselves treating our wives as scapegoats instead of helpmates. Some men use their wives as "whipping boys," blaming them when they fail to achieve great things in their lives. Others accuse their wives of being the reason they are not the wonderful, successful, and pleasant guy they think they would be if it weren't for her.

You can take the *Nabal Test* right now to see if he is bleeding through into your character:

- Are you harder or softer toward your spouse now than when you first got married?

- Are you more forgiving or less forgiving of your mate's weak areas this year than last year?

- Have you pigeonholed their personality as a nag, hag, or bag because of the past, even though they have repented of yesterday's sins?

- Do you appreciate their strengths or do you feel threatened by them?

- Do you expose your spouse's weaknesses or cover them?

Do you get the point? I found within my own life that I was developing an unhealthy attitude toward my wife. When she tried to communicate heart-issues with me, I did not hear what she was saying. Over and over, she would try to articulate what she meant but I did not hear a word. I had already reached my conclusions based on my Nabal-like perception of her.

Sometimes a lot of time and effort is needed in conversation before a "light bulb" finally turns on and we begin to understand. It is truly hard work, but when the light does come on, I find myself saying, "Oh, *that's* what you mean. *Now* I see where you are coming from!"

We may not like to admit that we have Nabal-like tendencies, but if unforgiveness is hardening our hearts and cutting off communication, the death of our marriage is imminent. Nabal's life and death illustrate how an unforgiving spirit leads to ruin. We will never hear what our mate is truly saying if we harbor resentment and unforgiveness about past sins for which our mate has already repented. Unforgiveness affects our hearing and it limits our ability to process information. *"You will keep on hearing, but will not understand; you will keep on seeing, but will not perceive"* (Matthew 13:14).

What Jesus Says About Forgiveness

In Matthew 18, Jesus uses a parable to teach about forgiveness. A parable is an earthly story that tells a heavenly truth. It is intended to give greater insight. Thus, a parable is to understanding what a window is to a room: it lets in light.

As Jesus taught on the subject of people who rub us the wrong way, Peter asked, *"Lord, how often shall my brother sin against me and I forgive him? Up to seven times?"* (Matthew 18:21). Peter probably thought, "Pretty impressive for me to forgive the same person for the same offense seven times in one day."

To tell you the truth, I am impressed.

Consider this example: an acquaintance says to you, "I've been gossiping about you with a bunch of people at work, please forgive me." So you forgive him. An hour later, he calls and says, "I'm down here at the gym. One thing led to another and I started slandering you to the people down here. Please forgive me."

Now you're thinking, "What is this guy's problem?" Wanting to be spiritual, you say, "Okay, I forgive you," but then you add, "Watch what you say, though; you're ruining my reputation." Forty-five minutes later he calls again and says, "Please forgive me. I ran into the market to get some milk, and when I got to talking in the check-out line, I started criticizing you."

At this point, I would probably lose my cool, question his sincerity, and sarcastically tell him, "You know, I used to be an angel until backbiters like you chewed off my wings! No, I will not forgive you. I never want to see your face again!"

Keeping that scenario in mind, I am impressed with the ability of Peter to forgive the same person for the same offense seven times in one day. But Jesus is not impressed. He says to Peter, *"I do not say to you, up to seven times, but up to seventy times seven"* (v. 22). In other words, don't keep score. We are not to be like those who keep a record of how often they have been offended and how often they forgave. Jesus is saying it is not a matter of mathematics but of attitude. Have a heart of forgiveness.

To illustrate, Jesus taught this parable:

For this reason the kingdom of heaven may be compared to a king who wished to settle accounts with his slaves. When he had begun to settle them one who owed him ten thousand talents was brought to him. [That is about $10,000,000 – an impossible debt to pay. Bill Gates was not around, nor were millionaires among the general population.] *But since he did not have the means to repay, his lord commanded him to be sold, along with his wife and children and all that he had, and repayment to be made.*

– Matthew 18:23-25

In other words, justice was to be meted out in the situation. It was a fair penalty. It might not seem like a very kind thing to do, but legally it was the just thing to do.

Notice the response from the one who owed the debt (v. 26):

So the slave fell to the ground and prostrated himself before him, saying, "Have patience with me and I will repay you everything."

The servant acknowledged his guilt and stated his willingness to make restitution.

Recognizing our sin and being willing to change is pleasing in the Lord's eyes. Notice in verse 27 that his lord *"...felt compassion and released him and forgave him the debt."* But then, in verse 28, *"That slave went out and found one of his fellow slaves who owed him a hundred denarii; and he seized him and began to choke him, saying, 'Pay back what you owe.' "* Here the slave who had been forgiven by his master is now facing the same scenario with a fellow slave. The cause was just. His fellow slave did owe him, albeit a minuscule amount compared with his own debt to the master. A hundred denarii amounted to about fourteen weeks' wages, therefore, in this case, it would have been possible to pay off the debt by means of indentured service.

So his fellow slave fell to the ground and began to plead with him, saying, "Have patience with me and I will repay you." But he was unwilling and went and threw him in prison until he should pay back what was owed.

The one who was forgiven by his lord of a huge debt was now unwilling to forgive his fellow servant of a tiny debt. Instead, he threw him into prison until he paid it all. But how can you pay a debt if you are locked up? You can't! This is an example of holding a grudge and keeping it locked away to revisit whenever the urge strikes. It illustrates revenge and unforgiveness at its worst.

So when his fellow slaves saw what had happened, they were deeply grieved and came and reported to their lord all that had happened. Then summoning him, his lord said to him, "You wicked slave, I forgave you all that debt because you pleaded with me. Should you not also have had mercy on your fellow slave, in the same way that I had mercy on you?" And his lord, moved with anger, handed him over to the torturers until he should repay all that was owed him. My heavenly Father will also do the same to you, if each of you does not forgive his brother from your heart.

Do you know what makes the Lord angry? An unforgiving spirit. The parallels of this story are evident: the debt owed by the first servant was impossible to pay, yet when he repented, the master forgave him.

We are that slave, unable to pay our debt of sin to God. If we owned a universe of gold and mined it for eternity to pay our debt, it would not be enough. So God took it upon Himself to pay the price for us by the blood of His Son, Jesus.

Take a moment...

One slave *swallowed* his pride; the other *wallowed* in it. Which one are you? Do you need to make a change?

The Bible says, *"Knowing that you were not redeemed with perishable things like silver or gold from your futile way of life inherited from your forefathers, but with precious blood, as of a lamb unblemished and spotless, the blood of Christ"* (1 Peter 1:18-19). Only the blood of Jesus Christ shed on Calvary is sufficient to pay our debt.

What does it cost you to forgive the sins of others, especially your spouse? Have you locked your mate away in a spiritual prison from which there is no hope of escape or ever being forgiven? What would it cost you to forgive them? A little bit of pride? A little bit of ego? A little bit of humility? Remember Nabal? He was unwilling to forgive, and it cost him dearly.

In our parable, the Lord turned that wicked servant over to the torturers until all was paid. It does not appear the Lord is talking about a believer losing their salvation, but it definitely speaks of him living in a "hell on earth." An unforgiving spirit will "eat the life" out of a person. It will torment them every waking hour and bring suffering in the night, as they toss and turn on their bed of bitterness. It will age them before their time, crippling their mental faculties, and torturing them from the inside out.

Defeat the Past

We have looked at two of the enemy's strategies: first, how he uses less-than-ideal beginnings to make a couple doubt God's providence in bringing them together; and second, how he persuades one spouse to hold a grudge over sins from the past of which their mate has repented, keeping them in a prison of unforgiveness. These issues stop us dead in our marital tracks, rendering us unable to grow or go on with the plan God has for our marriage.

For those of you who have not had a great beginning, accept the fact that God's sovereign hand is on your marriage. The providence of God has brought you thus far and will lead you on. Your story may not be as extreme as that of David and Bathsheba, but be assured that no matter what the circumstances were, the sovereign and providential hand of God has always been upon you.

Remember Job? At first, he viewed his adversity as a sign that God was against him. The truth finally surfaced that God was on Job's side all along, working all things together for good. It just took time. At the end of Job's life, he was blessed twice as much as at the beginning. He came to understand that his trials were not forever and his condition of adversity was not permanent; God allowed those circumstances to exist with a view to a glorious future.

Do not give up. God is working good out of what may seem so bad. When the purposes of God were realized in Job's life and God had blessed him beyond his wildest dreams, he said in essence, "Well, shut my mouth!" More accurately, we read in Job 42:3, *"Surely I spoke of things I did not understand, things too wonderful for me to know"* (NIV).

The providence of God has brought you and your mate together. Now in order to move on and receive His blessing upon your marriage, you have to defeat the past by forgiving your mate.

Regarding forgiveness, apply this three-fold principle:

- First, the one guilty of sinning against the other should have a *repentant* heart, not an *expectant* heart. In other words, be more concerned with your own repentance – being truly sorry – than expecting forgiveness from your mate. (It will come in time, but true repentance does not look for conditions.)
- Second, the one who was wronged must be willing to forgive and to cultivate an attitude of forgiveness.
- Third, the couple needs to believe and apply all of God's promises concerning themselves and their situation. So read your Bible and see what He has for you.

LET'S DISCUSS
DEFEATING THE PAST...

1. Do you think it's more difficult to forgive or to forget?

    Is it possible to forgive without forgetting?

2. How does holding on to resentment over past offenses alter the way a person views his or her mate?

    How can that keep a marriage from moving forward?

3. Why do you think we find it so difficult to forgive?

    What does forgiveness cost us?

4. Who suffers from unforgiveness: the one who needs forgiveness or the one who is unwilling to forgive?

    Now consider, what do we gain when we forgive and forget?

Let's Apply What We've Learned...

1. Does your mate commit any offenses that stand out in your mind because of their *frequency*?

   Now...take a minute and consider how your mate would answer that same question about *you*. Does that change your perspective about forgiveness?

2. How can the ongoing consequences of sin make it difficult to forgive and forget?

3. Even if we sincerely repent, there may be things in our lives that raise doubt in our spouse's mind. If this is an issue in your marriage:

   a. What are you doing that might cast doubt upon your repentance?

b. What steps can you take to prove your sincerity?

4. Read the following passages, then answer the questions.

Isaiah 43:18

Jeremiah 31:34

Hebrews 10:17

Romans 5:8

a. How does God see our past sins?

b. If you haven't forgotten what you claim to have forgiven, what steps will you take now to view those past sins the way God does?

CHAPTER THREE

UNWITTING TOOLS OF THE ENEMY

*Have you found honey? Eat only as much as you need,
lest you be filled with it and vomit.*
— Proverbs 25:16 NKJV

They can be a great blessing to your marriage, but sometimes they can also be unwitting tools in the hands of the enemy, disrupting your relationship in ways you would never have expected. Who are "they"?

Your children, your in-laws, and your friends.

Maybe you have heard the expression "getting too much of a good thing." Proverbs 25:16 illustrates this point. We all like sweets, but having them in excess is sickening. The enemy works subtly in our lives through things that bring joy, pleasure, and sweetness. We all want to live "happily ever after" with family and friends, but there are times when even the sweetest things in life can turn bitter. We are blind-sided when the enemy uses those who are closest to us to strike at us.

I. Dividing Over Your Kids

Psalm 127:3 says, *"Behold, children are a gift of the Lord, the fruit of the womb is a reward."* How can what God intends to be a gift turn out to be so hard on the marital relationship? Kids can definitely put a major strain on a marriage, and the Devil will attempt to use them to bring division.

That innocent baby you brought home from the hospital goes from the "terrible twos" to the "terrifying teens" in no time. There are seasons along the road to adulthood where these "gifts of the Lord" seem more like *beasts from the abyss*! How can children, who are supposed to be the joy of our lives, turn into such trials for our marriages? What preventative measures can be taken so children remain a *pleasure* and do not add more *pressure* to the marital relationship?

Isaac and Rebekah: A Picture-Perfect Romance...Until

The story of Isaac and Rebekah in Genesis 24 is a beautiful tale of love, romance, and divine guidance. Abraham was not willing for his son Isaac to marry someone from among the women of Canaan, the land in which they were living, so he sent a servant back to his homeland of Mesopotamia to find Isaac a wife. The servant ended up at a well outside the city of Nahor where he prayed:

> *And he said, "O LORD, God of my master Abraham, grant me success today, I pray thee, and show steadfast love to my master Abraham. Behold, I am standing by the spring of water, and the daughters of the men of the city are coming out to draw water. Let the maiden to whom I shall say, 'Pray let down your jar that I may drink,' and who shall say, 'Drink, and I will water your camels' – let her be the one whom thou hast appointed for thy servant Isaac. By this I shall know that thou hast shown steadfast love to my master."*
>
> – Genesis 24:12-14 NRSV

It happened exactly as he had prayed. Rebekah, a shepherdess, appeared at the well and Abraham's servant asked her for a drink of water. She replied, *"Drink, my lord ... I will draw also for your camels until they have finished drinking"* (vv. 18-19). The servant thought it was too easy and wondered if he should get further confirmation, but finally he realized that the Lord had answered his prayer. After divulging his mission to Rebekah, they went to meet her father and mother. The servant explained his mission once again to the family, and they gave Rebekah the choice of going with the man or not. She felt God was directing her to go, so she left her family and began the journey to meet her husband-to-be.

As they neared the land of Abraham, Rebekah lifted up her eyes and saw a man in the distance walking in the field. (Isaac had gone into the field to meditate.) She inquired of the servant, "Who is that man walking in the field to meet us?" He replied, "It is Isaac, my master's son, the one you are to marry." Rebekah veiled her face in an act of modesty, dismounted her camel, and went out to meet Isaac.

Picture the romantic encounter: it's almost like that well-known commercial: *Two people in a flowery meadow run toward each other in slow motion and then embrace, spinning around and around as they kiss. Somehow, we know they will live happily ever after.*

But that is not exactly how this story goes. It certainly began with love, romance, and Divine guidance. After the heart-throbbing introduction in the field, Isaac took Rebekah, married her, and loved her. But then parenthood took its toll on the story's "happily ever after" ending.

From Romance to Rug-Rats

Isaac and Rebekah's passionate beginning had all the makings of a romance novel until the birth of their twins radically changed everything. When Esau and Jacob were born, they were rivals as well as twins. Esau was the rugged, individual type; he was a hunter, an outdoors man, rough, hairy, and known by his odor. His macho persona made him the favorite of his father. Brother Jacob, on the other hand, was quite different. He was the delicate, doting type. He loved to bake and hang out with Mom in the tent, and so he became her favorite. As the boys' personalities developed, the house became divided: one boy was soft and mellow, cooking in the kitchen with Mom, while the other was gruff and rugged, hunting in the field for Dad.

Tension began to build between Jacob and Esau. It happens in the best of homes no matter what the sex or age of the children. It is called *sibling rivalry*. It is easy for a parent to fall into the trap of choosing the side of their favorite child.

One day Esau came in from the field, his stomach growling and mouth watering as he smelled the aroma of a pot of stew Jacob was cooking (Genesis 25:29). After some bartering, Esau traded Jacob his birthright for a bowl of stew. (The birthright belonged to the firstborn. It was his privilege to carry on the heritage of God's blessings.)

So we start to see some flaws in the character of Esau. He is indifferent to the things of God, treating his birthright as though it was nothing (Genesis 25:29-34). Later on, Esau got involved with some Hittite women, pagans who *"brought grief to Isaac and Rebekah"* (Genesis 26:35). Still, Esau is the favorite son of Isaac, and in spite of his faults, his father wants to bless him.

When Isaac was old and almost blind, he told Esau, *"Please take your gear, your quiver and your bow, and go out to the field and hunt game for me; and prepare a savory dish for me such as I love, and bring it to me that I may eat, so that my soul may bless you before I die"* (Genesis 27:3-4). While Isaac was speaking, Rebekah was eavesdropping. When Esau left to carry out his father's instructions, Rebekah conspired with her favorite son Jacob to deceive Isaac and steal Esau's blessing.

Many times, Satan's strategy begins with a division in the home over the children. Whenever one child is favored above another, the enemy comes in and creates confusion and discord. And favoritism in a household does not have to be spoken; it can be readily felt. Remember, *"God is no respecter of persons"* (Acts 10:34 KJV). We should also be impartial.

Take a moment...

Can you think of any situations when your children have instigated conflict between you and your mate? How can you counteract those attempts at manipulation?

Deception Grows

This was not the first time deception had been committed in the family of Isaac. The seeds of duplicity were sown during a time of famine, when Isaac and Rebekah traveled to Gerar, where there was reported to be an abundance of food. Isaac was afraid Rebekah's beauty would get him killed. (Local sheiks were in the habit of expanding their harems with beautiful women, even if it meant murdering their husbands.) So Isaac told King Abimelech that Rebekah was his sister. It saved his hide but put his wife in great danger.

One afternoon, Abimelech looked out his window and saw Isaac caressing Rebekah. The king confronted him about his deception, saying, *"Behold, certainly she is your wife! How then did you say, 'She is my sister'?"* (Genesis 26:9). Isaac confessed, saying that he was afraid he would be killed and his wife taken, because they were in a hostile land. Abimelech rebuked him, saying, *"What is this you have done to us? One of the people might easily have lain with your wife, and you would have brought guilt upon us"* (Genesis 26:10). Here we see a pagan king rebuking a man of God for his deception. Abimelech charged Isaac with putting Rebekah at risk and exposing his people to potential sin.

When Isaac entertained compromise, he failed as a husband to protect his wife, forcing her into the position of fending for herself. A husband can force his wife into a place of independence by leaving her vulnerable and unprotected; she feels she must look out for herself. This can cause division in the home. A woman wants to be protected. God has declared, *"Your desire shall be for your husband, and he will rule over you"* (Genesis 3:16).

The effect of Isaac practicing deceit and leaving Rebekah at risk and unprotected created a breach in their home. It put Rebekah on her guard from that point on, whether she was conscious of it or not. Now, when she overheard the plan of Isaac to bless Esau, she schemed with Jacob to deceive his father and steal the blessing because, once again, she felt unprotected. She knew the will of God but did not trust the judgment of her husband, so she acted independently.

Take a moment...

Has a lack of trust introduced deception into your marriage? What can you do to repair the breach?

She told Jacob, in effect, "Go in and pretend you are your brother Esau in order to steal the blessing." But Jacob said, *"Behold, Esau my brother is a hairy man and I am a smooth man. Perhaps my father will feel me"* (Genesis 27:11-12). Rebekah then instructed Jacob to take an animal skin and wrap it around his hands and neck so that when Isaac felt him he would seem hairy, like Esau. Jacob worried, *"I will be as a deceiver in his sight, and I will bring upon myself a curse and not a blessing"* (v. 12), but Rebekah insisted, *"Your curse be on me, my son; only obey my voice, and go ..."* (v. 13).

Jacob dressed in the garments of his brother to "smell the part," and covered himself with a hairy animal skin to feel the part if his father touched him. Then he went in to see Isaac, and greeted him, "My father." Isaac replied, *"Here I am. Who are you, my son?"* (v. 18). Jacob told his father, *"I am Esau, your firstborn; I have done as you told me. Get up, please, sit and eat of my game, that you may bless me"* (v. 19).

Then Isaac said to Jacob, *"Please come close, that I may feel you, my son, whether you are really my son Esau or not."* So Jacob came close to Isaac his father, and he felt him and said, *"The voice is the voice of Jacob, but the hands are the hands of Esau"* (v. 22). Then his father said to him, *"Please come close and kiss me, my son."* So Jacob came close and kissed him, and when Isaac smelled the scent of Esau's garments upon Jacob, he blessed Jacob. The deception was complete: Jacob stole the blessing of his father away from his brother. Shortly thereafter, Esau discovered the fraud and in a rage threatened to kill Jacob, but Rebekah hurriedly sent him away.

It is important to note that after Jacob left home there is no mention of him seeing his mother Rebekah ever again. This deception separated Jacob from his family for over twenty years, even though Rebekah told him in verse 44 "to stay away a few days until the anger of his brother subsided." When Jacob did return home, it was too late. Rebekah was dead. She lost the fellowship of her son as well as the trust and affection of her husband because *deception creates division.*

We can choose our sin, but we cannot choose its consequences. God is able to accomplish His purposes without our having to deceive in order to get His will done. Both Isaac and Rebekah were guilty of this and paid a heavy price for their folly.

Age-Old Principles for Parenting

There are lessons to be learned from the story of Isaac and Rebekah. What began as a *Cinderella love story* ended up as a train wreck, with one bad situation piling upon the next. The epilogue of their lives did not read, "And they lived happily ever after." Deep disappointment and overwhelming obstacles marked their lives. Theirs is not a model for successful marriage, but rather for *marital chaos.*

When examining their relationship, it becomes obvious that the enemy got to the parents through the children. Their marriage suffered because the children drove a wedge between father and mother. It can happen to any couple. Here are five principles for building up the parent-child relationship that will help avoid a marital train wreck.

Never Divide Over Your Children

Sometimes division can take place over disciplining the children. One parent might believe the other parent is too hard or too soft. Or perhaps there is a conflict over the *method* used in discipline.

From toddler to teenager, when one parent sides with the child against the other parent, division is inevitable. Remember, your children are with you only temporarily. One day they will leave, and you and your spouse will be left to "pick up the pieces" for the rest of your lives together.

What you sow you shall also reap. If you let the kids be a source of division, when they are grown and gone, you will reap an empty nest of blank stares across the breakfast table. If there have been years of division, deception, and a breakdown in trust, as in Isaac's family, you may end up a bitter couple.

Always Show a United Front

Children have an uncanny ability to sense the weakest link in the family chain. If Dad is a pushover in one area, they will get him on their side, contending with Mom. If Mom is the easy one, they will team up against Dad. Children know how to divide parents in order to get their own way. What takes place between a husband and wife in front of the children is a key factor in sending the right message to them. A lack of unity exposes those weak links that can later be exploited by the child. Always show a united front.

Never Disagree with Your Spouse in Front of the Children

If you have a conflict with each other over the method of discipline for your children, discuss it behind closed doors. **Never** disagree in front of the children. If one parent gives permission to the child for some activity and then the other parent chimes in opposing that decision, an argument will invariably ensue in front of the child. This is forbidden. Any disagreement should be carried out away from the listening ears of the children.

Do Not Let Your Children Force You to Choose Sides

Solve problems but do not choose sides. Children seek approval, sometimes over and against other family members. They tell their side of the story about the terrible thing that has happened, hoping you will side with them against their sibling or even against the other parent. Resist the urge to choose sides and instead just solve the problem.

Do Not Let the Devil Confuse the Real Issue

God is not the author of confusion but Satan is, and he seeks to confuse issues. A parent may be convinced that havoc in the home is a result of out-of-control children, but while it is true that kids go through periods of rebellion, there is an underlying issue. Satan comes to steal, kill and destroy, and the home is his primary target. Pray for wisdom; you cannot fight him with natural weapons.

For the weapons of our warfare are not of the flesh, but divinely powerful for the destruction of fortresses.

– 2 Corinthians 10:4

Remember that you can do much after you pray; but until you pray, you cannot do anything *but* pray. So pray with your mate regularly over the issues in the home.

When Parenting Philosophies Collide

What happens when each parent has a different philosophy on discipline? The Bible must be the standard in the home. There is room for discussion as to the appropriateness, severity, and type of discipline, but the bottom line is, it must be biblical.

Proverbs 13:24 states, *"He who withholds his rod hates his son, but he who loves him disciplines him diligently."* A parent who cannot say no to their child, or who refuses to discipline him because "I love them too much" reveals an insecurity in the parent-child relationship. You are really saying, "I do not want to offend my child and make him or her mad at me." This non-offensive approach in dealing with the child will come back to haunt both of you. It will create an emotionally-challenged child who, as an adult, will have difficulty functioning in the real world, which is full of disappointments and setbacks. If you do not discipline your children in love at an early age, the world will do it for you, often with harsh and devastating consequences.

It is vitally important that parents have a plan for child rearing. If the boundaries are not drawn and agreed upon by both parents early in the marriage, you will find yourselves making them up as you go, which can be confusing and erratic for the child. Remember, you are investing in them now as children, striving for a consistency in behavior that will "bear good fruit" when they are adults.

You cannot allow discipline to be haphazard, undefined, or a once-in-a-while kind of thing. Be consistent, be unified, and be clear about what is expected in the home and what the consequences of disobedience will be. This is not a code of cold, harsh rules written with an iron pen on the walls of the home, but rather nurturing principles communicated from the heart of a loving parent to the heart of the child. This in turn will cultivate love and respect for authority.

Unconditional love must be communicated when discipline takes place, whether it's a verbal correction or corporal punishment for willful rebellion.

II. Leaving and Cleaving

As we examine the problem of spiritual warfare in the home, we need to look at the subject of in-laws. You may have wonderful in-laws that you love dearly, or they might seem more like outlaws, sent to raid your happy home. Whether you adore or abhor them, the Bible tells us in Genesis 2:24, *"For this reason [marriage] a man shall leave his father and his mother, and be joined to his wife; and they shall become one flesh."* We are instructed to leave Mom and Dad when we get married.

Jacob and Rachel

We can learn a lot about God's wisdom in leaving and cleaving from the story of Jacob and Rachel.

Jacob fell in love with Rachel, the beautiful daughter of Laban, in Genesis 29. Because of his respect for her father, Jacob agreed to work seven long, hard years to earn Rachel's hand in marriage, which because of his love for her, seemed *"but a few days"* (Genesis 29:20). Jacob's actions were honorable, showing gratitude and esteem for his future in-laws.

Seven years later, the wedding night finally arrived. Laban brought the veiled bride into the darkened wedding tent. The marriage was consummated, but the next morning Jacob awoke to a surprise: the bride was not Rachel but her older sister Leah.

Jacob shouted to Laban, "You deceived me! I worked seven years for Rachel. She is the love of my life. Instead, you brought in Leah. Now I have consummated the relationship, and she is forced to be my wife!" (Since having intimate relations was tantamount to marriage, there was no turning back; so Jacob did the honorable thing in staying married to Leah.)

Laban explained, "Were you not aware that in this part of the country, we never give the younger daughter in marriage first? The older one is always the first to marry. I am surprised you did not know that custom. But if you really want Rachel, work for me another seven years and I will give her to you." Jacob agreed, and Laban gave Rachel to him right away, without waiting until his second seven-year servitude was over.

Parents have a natural affection for their children and an innate desire to look out for their welfare, but Laban shows how fatherly instincts can interfere with and hinder the children's happiness. Parents may have the best intentions of wanting to treat their child and their child's mate equally, but the truth is the welfare of their own child will always supersede that of their son or daughter-in-law.

Laban secured the welfare of his own daughters at the expense of his good name; honesty and integrity took a back seat. He saw that Jacob was a good man, so he took advantage of him for the benefit of his daughter Leah.

This is an extreme example, but the principle stands. Your in-laws have their child in the deepest part of their heart, and although you have become part of the family, they will always want to make sure that *their* little girl or boy is happy.

Jacob stayed with Laban for twenty years. He did not *leave and cleave* as the Bible instructs. You might be thinking that Jacob's circumstances were out of the ordinary. That was true in the beginning, but then Jacob chose to live six additional years with his in-laws for financial reasons. It created much strife in the home.

In-laws sincerely want the best for their children but sometimes tend to interfere in their lives. Good intentions can easily lead to unwelcome meddling.

Problems are mounting in Jacob's household: jealousy between the wives, strife among the cousins, and animosity between him and Laban. Finally, Jacob tells his in-laws, "Things are too difficult. It is time for us to go." From Laban's point of view, however, things could not be better. He has twelve grandchildren around him, a hard-working son-in-law, and no "empty nest syndrome" to deal with. But Jacob has had it. He wants out.

Motivated by his own selfishness, Laban tries to persuade Jacob to stay longer. Distrust between them runs high. When Laban pleads with Jacob to stay a few more years, Jacob agrees; but now whenever he makes plans to leave, Laban tries to make him feel guilty. He accuses Jacob of using their relationship to increase his own personal wealth. But Jacob reminds him, *"You had little before I came, and it has increased to a multitude"* (Genesis 30:30). Clearly, Laban has benefited from Jacob's years of service.

Resentment and suspicion continue to grow between them. Jacob agrees to stay longer but expresses his inherent mistrust of Laban: *"My honesty will answer for me later, when you come concerning my wages"* (v. 33). In other words, "I don't trust you. When I prosper, you will protest and accuse me of cheating you in order to extort from me what I have honestly earned."

As time passes, Laban's sons' suspicion grows. In Genesis 31:1, they accuse Jacob of taking away the wealth of their father. The relationship sours; no longer are family members on friendly terms. Jacob is called a thief and Laban is branded a cheat. Jacob and his family end up sneaking away at night without even saying good-bye to the in-laws.

As they pack their bags to leave, Rachel steals the family idols. Three days later, when Laban discovers the images missing, he overtakes Jacob and charges him with theft.

They almost exchange blows as Laban accuses him: *"Why did you flee secretly and deceive me, and did not tell me so that I might have sent you away with joy and with songs, with timbrel and with lyre; and did not allow me to kiss my sons and my daughters?"* (vv. 27-28). Then he tells Jacob that his household gods are missing and he suspects his son-in-law of taking them. (It must be sad to serve gods that can be stolen!)

Meanwhile Rachel, acting oh so innocent, has hidden the statues in her saddlebag and is sitting on them. After Laban searches Jacob and Leah's tents along with the two maids, he comes to Rachel's tent. He looks all around but does not find them. Rachel asks him to forgive her for not getting up off her saddle, using the excuse that she is having her menstrual period. The lie prevents Laban from finding the idols in her saddlebag.

Talk about dysfunctional families! This brood has really turned on one another. Why? Jacob failed to heed God's precept: "leave your mother and father and cleave to your wife, and the two shall become one flesh."

Finally, Laban and Jacob make a covenant, piling up stones as a memorial and saying, *"This heap is a witness between you and me this day... May the Lord watch between you and me when we are absent one from the other"* (vv. 48-49). A beautiful tribute? No! It is an expression of animosity and distrust, saying in essence, "May God watch my back, because He knows I can't trust a rotten thief like you."

Needless to say, they parted company on the worst of terms, still suspicious of each other. What God meant for good, Jacob and Laban ruined because they did not observe the principle of leaving and cleaving.

Marriage has what is known as an *Inner Circle* relationship. Picture a target with a bull's eye in the center and consecutive circles moving outward. The bull's eye is the inner circle, where we deal with our personal problems, financial matters, the discipline of our children, communication problems, and other issues relating to the family core. The only people who are allowed to enter the inner circle are you, your spouse, your children, and God. All others must be invited by mutual consent of the husband and wife.

As a pastor, if I am to counsel a couple, I need to be invited to do so by both parties. If I give counsel based only on one person's side, I violate their partner who has not invited me into that inner circle.

Laban jumped into Jacob's inner circle, and Jacob let him stay there, creating long-term problems.

Take a moment...

Is there anyone in your Inner Circle without your mate's knowledge or permission?

What It Means to Leave

When God tells us to leave, it means more than simply stepping out of our parents' home and into a new one with our mate. Leaving encompasses other areas that, if neglected, can disrupt God's plan for marriage.

We Must Leave Financially

Sometimes couples feel as if they need financial aid from their in-laws in order to survive. As a rule, it is better to struggle to make ends meet rather than depend upon in-laws for financial help. It can be very convenient to be helped until you "get on your feet," but this can create a dependence upon the in-laws instead of upon the Lord. Most in-laws had to struggle when they first got married. That struggle created a sense of self-reliance and God-dependency, which all fledgling families need. Proverbs 16:26 expresses this well: *"A worker's appetite works for him, for his hunger urges him on."*

Laban had excessive influence on Jacob's family because he held the purse strings. In other words, he practiced the world's *golden rule*: "He who has the gold rules."

We Must Leave Physically

I have counseled couples where the husband has said, "Let's live with my parents for a short time until we get some money saved, and then we will find our own place." The wife agrees, and ten years later, they are still with his parents. They now have children, have no money saved, the husband acts like a "momma's boy," and the wife is completely frustrated. What is more, her parenting skills are in jeopardy because the children cannot decide if Mother or Grandmother is the final authority.

It is too easy for well-meaning parents to meddle in the affairs of their married children. It happens with disciplining the children, marital squabbles, money woes, and even meal preparation when they all live under the same roof. The in-laws tend to be the *masters* and the newlyweds the *apprentices*. This sets in motion a tendency for the masters to show the apprentices how it is done.

I was asked for counsel by a couple who were living with his parents. He was a surfer who unfortunately liked to surf more than he liked to work. So they never had enough money to become independent of his parents. (But then why should he when his parents paid the bills?)

His wife eventually became frustrated by this living situation. Her mother-in-law insisted on raising the grand-children as she had raised her own children. This invariably led to repeated clashes. The wife, in exasperation, finally packed her bags, took the children, and left her husband.

Long before it happened, we warned them of the inevi-table consequences of not *leaving and cleaving*. He ignored all the danger signals and surfed himself into a broken marriage. He shunned the responsibility of providing for his own family and instead relied upon Mom and Dad to do what he should have done. Ultimately he lost his wife and children.

We Must Leave Spiritually

Every couple must "own Christ" for themselves. They must chart their own spiritual course. This may involve walking in a different spiritual direction than their parents. You may have a strong spiritual heritage, which is a great advantage, but parents should not pressure their newlywed children into adopting the same church, pastor, or body of believers. It is healthy and needful for the children to make their own spiritual decisions. If the in-laws belong to a living, vibrant, Bible-teaching church, the newlyweds will likely gravitate there. If they do not, it is good that the young couple develop their own spiritual roots where they can grow in the things of the Lord.

We Must Leave Emotionally

Some people come from a family where strong ties and deep emotional bonds have been successfully built into the children. Caution needs to be taken so that the close parent-child bond does not interfere when marital disagreements arise. "My mate is too hard to talk to, so I am going to see what Mom and Dad have to say." That might sound innocent, but if it becomes a pattern, the husband and wife will never fully form their own emotional bond, and they will not develop problem-solving skills.

As a married person, you need to transfer your emotional support from your parents to your spouse. Parental wisdom can be a great help, but if your emotional stability still comes from them, a transfer over to your mate needs to occur.

Relating to Your Parents and In-Laws

Here are some principles to keep in mind as a married person when dealing with both your in-laws and your own parents.

Never Allow Your Parents Or In-Laws to Criticize Your Mate

At one time, my mother did not like my wife. That is probably the case with many mothers. They think that their son can do no wrong and that there is not a girl in the world who is good enough for him. My mother used to make snide remarks about my wife Danita, pointing out her faults and weaknesses. Before I became a Christian, I let it go, often even agreeing with the put-downs. Danita felt belittled and defensive. After I became a Christian, I realized the subtlety of Satan's strategy. My mother may have pointed out legitimate weaknesses in my wife, but the effect was devastating in our home.

As a brand new believer, I began to realize that God had made me the priest, provider, and protector of my home. My eyes were opened to the fact that I could never allow anyone, even a close family member, to criticize my wife. So the next time my mother said something about Danita, I said, "Mom, I do not ever want to hear another criticism of my wife. It is divisive and something God does not want me to hear from you. So please do not do it again."

It was difficult to reprove my mother because I believe children should honor their parents, but I had allowed improper criticism to come in, due to my worldly ways, and because I was now a Christian, I had to deal with it.

The good that came out of it was a reborn relationship between my mother and my wife. As time went on, my mother confided that she felt Danita was her best friend and confidante. If I had let that criticism continue to go unchecked, their friendship would have never developed the way it did.

Never Allow Your Parents or In-Laws to Make Decisions for Your Family

Inner circle decisions need to be made by you, your mate, and the Lord, counseling together to decide upon a course of action. You can seek advice from your in-laws, if you both agree to do so, but you should not allow your parents to impose their decisions upon you.

Never Allow Your Parents or In-Laws to Overrule Your Decisions Concerning Your Children

Issues relating to your children can include discipline, eating habits, privileges, schedules, television watching, and so on.

Friends of ours, who have a marriage ministry, tell of a time after their first child was born that they went to Grandma and Grandpa's house. The little guy was acting up, and Dad said, "You are going to get a spanking if you do not behave."

Grandpa picked up the boy and declared, "You will never spank my grandson in my home!" Dad went over, took the boy out of Grandfather's arms, and said, "Then your grandson will never be in your home." Mom and Grandma were in the kitchen on "pins and needles" as they heard the commotion. The husband called to the wife, "Come on, we are leaving!" And they left. It was a tearful situation.

The Christian husband felt his inner circle was being violated and that he had to make a decision. He thought, "If I do not take a stand in this situation, my in-laws may feel free to disregard other decisions my wife and I make and take free reign in our home."

Fortunately, the grandfather called back about an hour later and apologized. The relationship was restored and as a result was better than ever.

Enjoy your parents and in-laws, but realize that there are boundaries. You, along with your spouse, your children, and the Lord are a unique family unit. Parents can offer sound wisdom and advice but should never impose it upon you.

Take a moment...

Have you allowed your in-laws to interfere with your marriage in the areas of: family planning, finances, child rearing, conflict resolution, respect or emotions? How can you re-establish boundaries?

III. Your Friends –
The Danger in a Whisper

A perverse man spreads strife, and a slanderer separates intimate friends.

— Proverbs 16:28

Friends can divide a marriage. They can be well-meaning but whisper about things they should not, thereby sowing discord. Never allow a friend to speak negatively of your mate. We all fall short at one time or another, but a friend who seeks to console you by pointing out flaws in your spouse is doing damage to, and not repairing, the relationship. Never let friends criticize your mate.

Proverbs 17:9 says, *"He who conceals a transgression seeks love, but he who repeats a matter separates intimate [best] friends."* When problems occur within the marriage, friends can hinder instead of help when they offer criticism. A well-meaning but spiritually immature friend who sides with you against your mate is widening the breach instead of closing it. Friends who incite more frustration and anger toward your spouse are, in fact, meddling and separating intimate friends (you and your mate).

Be wise to the schemes of the Devil; he works subtly. If a friend causes you to think negatively of your mate, while at the same time making you feel closer to them, be alarmed. Perhaps your friend-turned-counselor has relationship problems of their own which remain unresolved. It may be a "misery loves company" scenario without either of you knowing it. In any event, when you agree with your friend against your mate it is a slippery downward slope. Do not allow it.

Maybe what happened to your friend in his or her marriage is now happening to you and they have "hit the nail on the head" regarding your mate's problem. Respond by saying, "Please pray for us. The Lord is going to really have to work in our lives." You need to trust Jesus; otherwise, you will find the enemy coming in and making the breach even wider through the agency of a well-meaning friend.

How to Hush the Whisper

Here is some practical help for married couples when dealing with friends.

Never Have Separate Friendships of the Opposite Sex

There is no reason to cultivate a friendship with the opposite sex outside of your marriage, and there is no reason not to bring your mate into already-existing relationships with the opposite sex after you are married. I have warned couples about this principle and have seen it take its toll on those who ignore it.

One couple in particular comes to mind. They are now divorced. The husband was a waiter at a popular restaurant in Hawaii and his wife complained that flirtatious girls would come up to him to initiate a friendship – he even seemed to encourage it. When his wife was in the restaurant, she would just stand silently in the background waiting for him. He never acknowledged her or introduced her to the other ladies.

"That is dangerous," I told them. "He needs to introduce you. If he knows a girl, if she is a friend, then he needs to grab you and say, 'Oh, by the way, this is my wife.' " Doing so allows "friends" of the opposite sex to know immediately that we have a mate that we love and with whom God has made us one flesh.

Take a moment...

Do you have any inappropriate friendships or internet relationships?

Would your mate agree with your answer?

Never Let Close Friends into Your Inner Circle

When it comes to protecting the inner circle, close friends are no different than parents and in-laws.

Never Participate in Gossip about Your Spouse

We need to be wise to the schemes of the Devil. The quickest way to erode a relationship is to hear and participate in negative remarks about your mate. Ill-advised friends will sometimes seek to console you by pointing out your spouse's faults. But as they get your blood boiling over what a "dirty bird" you are married to, this will only hinder and not help the situation.

We all want maximum enjoyment from our family, friends, and relatives, but it must not come at the expense of marital harmony. The people closest to us have a way of playing on our emotional heartstrings. They may not even know what they are doing – or then again, maybe they do. We need to be mindful of the strategy of the enemy, which is to take what is good and use it for evil. We cannot allow children to drive a wedge into the marital relationship, as they did with Isaac and Rebekah; neither should we let parental help turn into in-law headaches, as it did with

Laban and Jacob. Remember that your children are destined to leave home eventually and friends will come and go; only your mate stays permanently.

What lasts, what is permanent, is the relationship you build for the rest of your life with your husband or wife. Much of the enjoyment you experience will depend upon how you handle the other people and problems that pass through your life.

LET'S DISCUSS THE
UNWITTING TOOLS OF THE ENEMY...

1. What are some short-term and long-term consequences of favoring one child over another?

2. Consider the snowballing effect of Laban's deception.

   a. How would you feel if you were:

      Leah?

      Rachel?

      Jacob?

      Laban's grandchildren?

   b. How did Laban's deception affect their relationships?

   c. How does deception affect your relationships?

3. We may naturally get along better with one child, or perhaps have more likes and dislikes in common.

   a. What steps can you take in the home to ensure equality among your children? How can you maintain common ground with all your children?

   b. How can you tell if you are favoring a child? What are some signs of favoritism?

4. There may be many times in your life when you would benefit from wise counsel.

   a. At what point does external advice or counsel violate the Inner Circle?

   b. How can you benefit from seeking advice without allowing it to dictate your decisions?

LET'S APPLY WHAT WE'VE LEARNED...

1. Get together and briefly (in two paragraphs) write the story of your romance: how you met, how you married. If you like, you could share it with the group next week.

2. How might favoritism obstruct your ability to see God's truth in your home?

3. Do you make negative comments about your mate to anyone? Do you allow others to make negative comments about your mate in your presence?

    a. In the future, what will you do when you are tempted to gripe about your mate to someone else, or when others gripe about her/him to you?

    b. If there is anyone with whom you are particularly susceptible to complaining about your mate, what can you do to plug up that hole?

4. Diagram your family's inner circle—the way it should be, not necessarily the way it is. Any person there must be accountable to that family core.

    Consider this your family's written covenant.

CHAPTER FOUR

FIGHT THE GOOD FIGHT

Be angry, and yet do not sin; Do not let the sun go down on your anger.

— Ephesians 4:26

The Boxing Ring

I once heard Chuck Swindoll share this vivid illustration from his childhood, which provides a telling example of the enemy's strategy to divide marriages (or families):

> You'll be surprised to know, I grew up in a home next door to a boxing ring. That's right, ringside, every Saturday night. Preliminary bouts were held during weeknights, but the main event was always on Saturday night, late, somewhere between 11:30 and 1:00 in the morning. The fights were never fair. There was an 11-year-old bantamweight, a welter-weight dad, and a light-heavyweight mom. It was a scene.
>
> When the main event began, the three Swindoll kids would quickly gather in the boys' room, turn off the light, push open the window, and watch it all happen. My mother would put on the popcorn, and serve it up with Cokes and hot chocolate. I'll tell you, it was better than *Hawaii Five-O, Kojak, The Rockford Files,* and *The Dukes of Hazard* all rolled into one.

It was the best show in east Houston: always unpredictable, and always exciting. Frankly, I was sorry to see those folks finally move.

I wonder what folks who live around us might hear if they pushed open their windows and listened to what goes on in our households. We struggle to express ourselves, to get our point across, to make our feelings known. Communication is a difficult process and conflicts can easily arise. When I hear of couples who say, "You know, we have been married for thirty years, and we have never argued," I think to myself, "Do they ever see each other? Check their pulses. Have they been breathing for the last thirty years?"

I wish I could say that my wife and I have not argued for thirty days, much less thirty years, but I cannot. As we have matured in our relationship with Christ, we have learned to disagree constructively. Bickering has matured into impassioned discussions. As we have grown in Christ, we have learned how to have disagreements and still keep it biblical.

How do you have a "good fight" with your spouse and keep it *biblical*? For starters, fighting physically is totally out of bounds. A good fight is a verbal conflict where each partner has an opposing opinion. To keep a fight biblical means that you cannot fight "dirty."

I once saw an Olympic boxing match where one fighter thought the referee had called a time out, and so he walked back to his corner. His opponent thought otherwise, and ran up behind him and started slugging away, roundhousing in the side of his head, just about knocking him out. This is referred to as blind-siding your opponent – a "hitting-below-the-belt" technique. Mike Tyson was disqualified for trying to bite off Evander Holyfield's ear. Now that really is fighting dirty!

Many political opponents will "hit below the belt" when they are in a heated discussion. Even Christian couples will use sarcasm, spiteful words, and personal put-downs. Some couples I have counseled have confessed to getting into cursing matches. Even "moody silence" is a form of "hitting-below-the-belt." It is an icy quiet, filling the room with animosity.

I am very familiar with this kind of strategy because it happened in our home when I was growing up. My stepfather would fill the house with a "moody silence," creating an atmosphere of tension and gloom. It could last for several days. This is a cruel thing to do to children. It is very intimidating to come home to that kind of environment. My family members were not believers, but I know this even happens in Christian homes.

Why Couples Fight

Is it biblical to fight? Why do couples fight? Aren't Christian couples supposed to live *happily ever after*?

There are several reasons we get into conflicts and end up arguing. First of all, when couples are just beginning to get to know each other, they want to put their best foot forward, which can lead to varying degrees of phoniness. Second, before you get married there is really very little commitment. You can stay in the relationship or move on at any time. But once you get married, reality sets in. It is where "the rubber meets the road" in a relationship. In marriage there is no pretense. You have made a commitment. There is no bailing out, no getting into the car and driving off.

While you are dating, you may find it relatively easy to tolerate things you do not really like. You endure what you have to in order to win the affection of the other person. You even pretend to accept things that really bother you. Everything appears to be wonderful in the courtship stage.

I can recall some of my own *make-believe moments* back when I was dating my wife Danita. Her family did not have a washer and dryer, and with five people in her household, the laundry would rapidly pile up. Danita had to take the clothes to the Laundromat, so, being her boyfriend, I would go with her – sometimes for three hours or more. I wanted to spend time with her, but if you asked me about the waiting, the folding, the separating of the whites from the darks – the whole routine – I would tell you I hated it.

After we got married, she said, "Let's go down to the Laundromat and do the laundry." I let out a howl, showing my true feelings. "I thought you liked doing the laundry," she said. "No," I confessed, "I tolerated it, but I never liked it." Suddenly, reality shattered the make-believe.

It was much the same with my surfing. When we were dating I would go to the beach with Danita, and she would sit and watch while I surfed. After we were married, however, I'd say, "Come on, Sweetheart, let's go to the beach," and she would respond, "What am *I* going to do? I don't want to just sit on the beach and wait while you go surfing."

"I thought you liked going with me to watch me surf?!" I exclaimed. "You did when we were dating." She finally admitted: "I just tolerated it back then."

Make-believe romance cuts deeper than just laundry or the beach. For example, the guy may seem very assertive in leadership areas before marriage. He may appear to be a take-charge kind of guy spiritually and in other areas. So the woman thinks, "Wow, this is the kind of guy I've always wanted. He's great!" Then, after the wedding, he seems to *flake out* and she feels *faked-out*. "I thought he was such a leader," she moans. "I thought he would take charge, but now it seems he wants me to be his mother and take the lead."

Take a moment...

How did you "fake out" your mate early on in your relationship?

What have you stopped "tolerating" about your mate since you've been married?

In situations like these, it is easy to see how a relationship can become tangled up in conflict. The key is how we deal with these conflicts. Dirty fighting – using spiteful words and attacking each other's character – is a tool of the enemy; it will lead to the ruin of your marriage. The foundation is not going to collapse all at once, but the longer you allow dirty fighting to continue in your relationship, the weaker the foundation becomes.

The weakening of the foundation can be likened to a beachfront home. When storms come, huge waves wash up onto the shoreline. When they come in contact with the foundation of a house, erosion begins to take place. Eventually, the house collapses and falls into the water. This process does not happen all at once, it happens little by little.

We need to recognize that when two strong, independent personalities get together, a clash is inevitable – and that's okay. When two strong streams merge turbulence will occur at the point of convergence, and afterward a powerful river emerges downstream. To tame the flow and utilize the power, our marriages need the Word of God. Christian couples can go through conflicts and still be biblical in their behavior and attitudes. We need to learn how to stay in the Spirit when we have conflicts. If we stay in the Spirit while we work out our differences, we will actually draw closer together and become stronger as a couple.

Conflicts work like dynamite, which can be used either to *implode* or to *explode* a structure. When a building is imploded, it collapses into itself once the dynamite is detonated, as opposed to exploding out in all different directions. In the same way, the Devil wants to see a blowout in your marriage. He tries to use conflict as a detonator to divide and separate couples. God uses it to bring them closer together.

Biblical Principles for Dealing with Conflict

Ephesians 4:25-32 says:

Therefore, laying aside falsehood, speak truth, each one of you, with his neighbor, for we are members of one another. Be angry, and yet do not sin; do not let the sun go down on your anger, and do not give the devil an opportunity. He who steals must steal no longer; but rather he must labor, performing with his own hands what is good, so that he will have something to share with one who has need. Let no unwholesome word proceed from your mouth, but only such a word as is good for edification according to the need of the moment, so that it will give grace to those who hear. Do not grieve the Holy Spirit of God, by whom you were sealed for the day of redemption. Let all bitterness and wrath and anger and clamor and slander be put away from you, along with all malice. And be kind to one another, tender-hearted, forgiving each other, just as God in Christ also has forgiven you.

In this passage there are seven principles that, when applied to your marriage, will bring you closer together as a couple.

1. Be Truthful Toward Each Other

Therefore, laying aside falsehood, speak truth, each one of you, with his neighbor, for we are members of one another.

– Ephesians 4:25

It is important to be truthful and to honor each other. Zechariah 8:16 says, *"These are the things which you should do: speak the truth to one another; judge with truth and judgment for peace in your gates."*

When married couples discuss issues, there needs to be confidence that each is 100 percent honest with the other. Some couples marry and do not have this pledge of honesty. As the years go by, inconsistencies in their mate's truthfulness are discovered and distrust and suspicion build.

Once trust is broken, the enemy has a place to drive a wedge into your relationship. If this is the case in your marriage, it is time to agree together to always be honest with each other. Get alone and make a pact of truthfulness.

What does honesty in a relationship mean? Being truthful does not mean telling your mate every thought you have or ever temptation you encounter. As one fellow stated, "If I see a pretty girl while I'm out walking with my wife and I have an impure thought, should I tell my wife about it?" This is not what honesty in marriage means. Sometimes Satan will bring temptation our way, but we do not need to tell our mates every evil thing that the Devil throws at us or that our old nature conjures up.

The issue of honesty cuts deeper than just temporal, surface issues. It deals with our character, our very nature. We can literally choose to take on a dishonest personality. As Jeremiah 9:5 illustrates: *"Everyone deceives his neighbor, and does not speak the truth, they have taught their tongue to speak lies; they weary themselves committing iniquity."* Notice he says, *"They have taught their tongue to speak lies."*

When I was a kid, I was a great liar. I didn't have much parental guidance when I was growing up, so lying became an art. During the last week of high school, I cut classes with three friends to go on a surfing trip. When the school administration found out about my absence, the vice principal ushered me into his office.

"Where were you?" he asked. I looked him right in the eye and put on a mask of innocence. "I was at home watching my sister's kids."

"All right," he said. You are dismissed," and he waved me out of his office.

When he questioned the other three guys, they told the truth about going surfing. "Bill drove," they added, but the vice principal did not believe them. "I can respect somebody who can look me right in the eye and tell me the truth," he declared, speaking unwittingly about me. "You guys are lying."

Later on, however, he learned the truth. When he brought me back into his office he didn't even look at me. "You're out of here," he told me. "I stuck up for you, and now I realize that you lied to me." I got kicked out of high school the last week before graduation.

We either teach ourselves to lie or we teach ourselves to tell the truth. The choice is ours. When it comes to the marital relationship, some might think that because of a lack of understanding between a couple, there is good reason to "fudge" on honesty a bit, to shave the truth a little in order to have peace in the home. However, if you are a born-again Christian, you have a higher moral standard. You certainly do not want to lie against the truth and against the Holy Spirit. John 16:13 says:

> But when He, the Spirit of truth, comes, He will guide you into all the truth; for He will not speak on His own initiative, but whatever He hears, He will speak; and He will disclose to you what is to come.

As a believer, the Spirit of truth dwells in me, leading and guiding me into all truth. If I lie to my mate, I am grieving the Holy Spirit. My wife entrusts me to the Lord, so she knows that I will tell the truth. In the same way, I entrust her to the Lord, so I know she will tell the truth. I look to her relationship with Jesus as she looks to mine; He is the basis of our truthfulness.

We must also be without guile in our relationships. Jesus said of Nathanael, *"Behold, an Israelite indeed, in whom is no guile"* (John 1:47 KJV). A person with guile is someone who shades or hides the truth. Jesus looked at Nathanael and said, "There is no deceit in this man. He is not good at lying or hiding the truth."

I can say that about my wife Danita. There is no guile in her. She is extremely innocent and honest. Being without guile is an attribute we should all desire. Jesus says we must *"become like children"* (Matthew 18:3). Normally a child is without guile because they do not think in terms of deception.

Have you ever seen a little child try to hide something? They might have a golf ball in one hand and nothing in the other, and they will come and say, "Guess which hand the ball is in?" Of course, you pick the one that is obviously empty. Laughing jubilantly, the child squeals, "Here it is!" holding out the hand you had not chosen. "Wow, you really fooled me," you tell them. Children just do not understand deceit.

When my own son, Bud, was just a little guy, he got into a bag of miniature marshmallows and began heading out the front door with two big fistfuls. I was sitting in my easy chair reading and when I looked up, I could see traces of something white oozing out of his fists. "Hey, Bud," I said as he approached the door. He froze. "Come here. What do you have in your hands?"

"Nothing," he said.

"Let me see," I told him.

He raised up his fists with the miniature marshmallows sticking out of his fingers. "What have you got?" I asked.

He knew he was in trouble, so with a guilty half-smile and his little lisp he said, "Marthmallowths." He was so cute I let him have the marshmallows.

We need to follow the example of a child by not becoming good at deception. The Bible says: *"How blessed is the man to whom the Lord does not impute iniquity, and in whose spirit there is no deceit!"* (Psalm 32:2). You show honor to your mate when you are truthful.

Sometimes however, one spouse might do something incredibly hurtful to the other. After repenting to the Lord and to their mate, they wonder, "Why doesn't my partner forgive me?" Realize that it is not a matter of forgiveness but it is a matter of trust. Trust needs to be earned and built back up. It will not happen automatically; it takes time.

2. No Low Blows

Be angry, and yet do not sin.

– Ephesians 4:26

Notice that Paul is giving us permission to be angry but not to let anger lead us into sin. Sometimes people try to conceal their anger. They are like volcanoes ready to erupt, and when they finally do vent, they explode. We can become angry, but it should never lead us into a place of sin.

How do you know when your anger is sinful? I have talked with couples who throw things, break things, swear at each other, and punch the walls so badly they need patching. I would say these are examples of *anger unto sin*. Anger that controls a person is sinful. After this kind of behavior, you will have a lot of repairing to do – and not just to the walls and the furniture. You must be sorry for and repent of your actions to your mate.

Never use physical violence. If you hit your mate it will be extremely difficult, if not impossible, to get them back on your side. The Bible says in Proverbs 18:14: *"The spirit of a man can endure his sickness, but as for a broken spirit who can bear it?"* A person can endure physical sickness, but if you use verbal or physical abuse to crush the spirit of your spouse, they will have a difficult time recovering. Proverbs 18:19 says, *"A brother offended is harder to be won than a strong city, and contentions are like the bars of a castle"* (NKJV). Think about a greatly fortified city and what it would take to conquer it. It would be extremely difficult. However, Proverbs says it would be easier to conquer that city than to win back a mate who has been offended.

Couples are not to use low blows, which break the spirit of their mate. These spiteful words – which attack the person and not the problem – are forbidden.

If a person finds himself in the position of seeking to win back a crushed mate, he will likely do anything to get them back. Take heed, though, and do it for the Lord's sake – because it is right in His eyes – for that is the only pure motive with lasting results. Anything less and you will wind up slipping back into your old ways once you have won back your mate.

What we really need is change that lasts, and that comes from *godly sorrow*. Winning back a husband or wife that you have offended or severely hurt is a monumental task which takes time and great patience. It flows out of a life that has been legitimately touched by God.

It took me about a year to win back my wife. During this time I was not consciously thinking, "I am on a mission to win over my wife's heart." It happened indirectly because I began to seek God and to be the man He wanted me to be. Before I even knew the Scripture, it was a *seek-first-the-kingdom-of-God-and-His-righteousness* kind of experience. I realized that He was the only One worth living for; He was the truth. Every other avenue I had gone down led to a dead end.

I came to the Lord at a time when my marriage was on the rocks. At this point my wife trusted me about a far as she could throw me. But she watched my life and eventually she began to realize, "There is something different about him: he treats the children better and he acts differently. But I do not want to be in this marriage anymore. I do not want him, and I certainly do not want Jesus Christ."

Fortunately, God was working on Danita's heart at the same time He was working on mine. After about one year she received Christ into her life and we have been together ever since.

Take a moment...

Low blows > Anger > Eroded Trust

What pathway can you take to develop *greater* trust in your marriage?

Keep in mind that the factors we might identify in a couple to predict durability and longevity are not always that obvious. How in love they say they are, how much affection they show one another, how often they argue, or the things they argue about are not telltale signs for whether or not their marriage will last. Both couples who ultimately make it and those who do not look remarkably the same in the early stages of marriage, much like the wheat and tares that grow up together in Jesus' parable in Matthew 13:24-30.

Psychologists Cliff Notarius of Catholic University and Howard Markman of the University of Denver studied newlyweds over their first 10 years of marriage, and found a subtle but important difference at the beginning of the relationships. Among the couples who ultimately divorced, 10 out of every 100 comments made by one about the other were insults. On the other hand, with the couples who stayed together, only 5 out of 100 comments were negative putdowns.

They found that the gap magnified over the following decade, until couples heading downhill were flinging five times as many cruel and invalidating comments at each other as happy couples. "Hostile putdowns act as cancerous cells that, if unchecked, erode the relationship over time," says Notarius. "In the end, relentless unremitting nega-tivity takes control and the couple can't get through a week without major blowups."[12]

3. Always Resolve the Conflict

*Do not let the sun go down on your anger ... and do
not give the devil an opportunity.*
                                        – Ephesians 4:26-27

Do not let conflict continue without dealing with it. If you have an argument, agree on a time and place where you can talk it out (or sometimes even argue it out) and bring it to a resolution. Do not underestimate small conflicts because, left unresolved, they can turn into mushroom clouds of contro-versy. You might think an issue is minor and therefore not worth pursuing, but to your mate it is a festering sore that can turn into a cancer in your relationship. Remember, the Devil loves to cause schisms over unresolved conflict.

Maybe time constraints will not allow you to deal with an issue immediately, so you say, "We can't talk about this now," and your mate responds, "Oh, just forget about it." That's not good! You need to talk it out; otherwise, a subtle crack develops which in time can turn into a chasm. If you can't deal with the issue immediately, then and there set a time when you will be able to talk about it.

When you do not agree to resolve a conflict, it becomes one more brick in a wall that will eventually divide you from your mate. Each problem you leave unsettled becomes another brick, and over the months and years, you will find yourself walled off in isolation from each other.

Over the last few years, my wife and I have resolved every conflict that has arisen. I am not saying we have always come to an agreement, but the conflicts were dealt with and resolved – even if we resolved to disagree, agreeably.

Once you have come to a resolution – though perhaps not an agreement – there is a greater warmth in your heart and greater love for that person.

Does the verse *"Do not let the sun go down on your anger"* mean you literally have to stay up all night to settle the argument? Not necessarily, but if you do not resolve it that night, then plan on a time the next day or within that week to get together and sort it out. Do not let it get lost to time or forgetfulness.

4. Be Part of the Solution

He who steals must steal no longer; but rather he must labor, performing with his own hands what is good, in order that he will have something to share with him who has need.

– Ephesians 4:28

If I am an expert *critic*, skilled at reprimand, and this is all my wife ever hears, I am offering nothing of value to her. What is needed are solutions to the problems, a helping hand for the situation. If I only criticize her, she is going to dig her heels in and refuse to listen. She will think, "There he goes again, criticizing me. I can't do anything right. Nothing I do satisfies him." This becomes how we view each other; it becomes the pattern by which we live.

When you take issue with your mate, come with the intent to support and offer solutions. This verse in Ephesians does not deal with conflict; it deals with patterns in a person's life. Paul points out the fact that there are men in the Church who used to be thieves and are now Christians. He doesn't say: "Stop stealing! Stop being a thief! Robbing is wrong!" Instead he instructs them: "Now that you have stopped stealing, start doing something constructive: work with your hands so you can make some money and share your goods with those who are in need."

Christianity is often perceived as a bunch of *don'ts*, but in reality, there are a lot more *do's*.

We might want to take a test to evaluate our disposition and see how positive or negative we really are. Let's look at *A Day in the Life of You*. To illustrate, I will take the test and rewind my life back to the earlier years of my marriage.

After a day spent making surfboards, I would come home and ask, "Where are my surf trunks?"

"Where they always are," Danita would reply. "In the shower." So I would grab my trunks, put them on, and go surfing until sunset.

When it was too dark to see the waves, I would paddle in, come home, and ask, "Where is my dinner?" Danita would tell me, "I have been cleaning the house so I haven't had time to cook. The vacuum cleaner went on the blink; I've been trying to get it to work. And the kids have been driving me nuts."

"Well, I'm hungry," I would complain. "I've worked all day, and now I'm home and I want to eat!" *[To replay a day in my life is embarrassing. I recall how self-centered I was. The Lord has a way of showing us our true nature.]*

Danita had been taking care of three children all day. Have you ever been stuck in conversation with a two-year-old, a five-year-old, and a seven-year-old for ten hours? It's often less-than-stimulating for an adult. She also had to deal with broken appliances and a messy house. Yet there I was harassing her with, "Where's my dinner? You've had plenty of time to fix me something to eat."

Instead of complaining, I could have encouraged her by saying, "How did your day go, Sweetheart?" When she told me about her disastrous day, I could have calmed her down, saying, "Wow, that's radical. Sit down here and I'll cook the meal. I'll even do the dishes." Rather than piling on more problems or pointing out what she did not do, I could have lent a helping hand along with an understanding ear.

The checkbook, bank statements, and financial issues are often a source of stress and tension in the home – they were in ours – but couples can avoid an all-out war by offering solutions rather than criticism.

A typical spat over money can start out with the husband saying, "I notice you are wearing a new outfit. Why are you buying luxuries when we don't have the money?" She frowns and answers, "How am I supposed to know how much money we have? You keep the checkbook."

"I don't always figure it out to the penny," he tells her, "but I have a general idea of it in my head. You are always spending money on this and that without checking with me." And the situation starts becoming tense.

A better response might be, "Honey, why don't we work out a budget together? How about if we both plan not to spend over a certain amount because money is going to be tight this month?"

Colossians 3:9-10 says, *"Do not lie to one another, since you laid aside the old self with its evil practices, and have put on the new self who is being renewed to a true knowledge according to the image of the One who created him."* If there is something we don't think is right in our home, we are to put off the old man and put on the new. In other words, stop complaining about what is wrong and do something to help change the situation. Try to be encouraging and offer solutions, not just criticism.

5. Be Diplomatic

Let no unwholesome word proceed from your mouth, but only such a word as is good for edification according to the need of the moment, so that it will give grace to those who hear.

— Ephesians 4:29

The word *unwholesome* literally translates "rotten." We are not to let any rotten word come out of our mouth. It is never good to say whatever comes into your mind during a heated discussion, and it is unwise to act upon your feelings at those times. *Watch your tone and your tongue.*

Experts say communication actually has three components: words, tone of voice, and non-verbal cues. Only 7% of communication has to do with the actual words; 37% is in the tone of voice and 56% is in nonverbal body language.[13] All three work together to send an accurate message. Each one of the components needs to be consistent with the others in order to communicate effectively.

When expressing your thoughts and feelings to your mate, be sensitive and diplomatic. If you were called upon to negotiate with terrorists over the hijacking of a Boeing 747, how would you handle the mission? The release of the hostages is at stake! Would you talk to them the same way you do to your wife when the two of you have a problem? If so, would you want to be on the plane with the hostages? Would the negotiations end badly?

The point is to deal with your spouse diplomatically. Do you *provoke* or *pacify* when you communicate? Draw proper boundaries with your words, your tone of voice, and your body language, and stay within those parameters.

Take a moment...

What do you need to change about your own body language or tone of voice when you communicate with your husband or wife?

6. Never Make It Public

Let all bitterness and wrath and anger and clamor and slander be put away from you, along with all malice.

— Ephesians 4:31

Do not bring your disagreements into the public arena. Do not humiliate your mate in front of others.

A man will sometimes use sarcasm around his family and friends in order to put his wife in her place. Some women figure a public forum is the best place to embarrass their husbands into doing what they want. So they make snide remarks and put-downs for everybody to hear. When you do this in public, it's not your mate who looks bad — it's you!

As a Bible teacher, I need to be especially sensitive in this area. I have used personal situations with Danita and myself to illustrate points in my messages, but I always make sure the conflicts have been resolved first and that if anyone is going to bear the brunt of my jokes or be the "bad guy," it will be me and not her.

Take a moment...

Have you ever humiliated your mate in front of others? If so, why did you do it?

Have you ever apologized?

7. Help Clean Up the Mess

Be kind to one another, tender-hearted, forgiving each
other, just as God in Christ also has forgiven you.
— Ephesians 4:32

Jesus wants us to be tenderhearted and forgiving, just as God in Christ has forgiven us. With that in mind, when our mate falls into a pit, we are to help lift them out. Do not bury them! If they fail, do not finish them off. Help restore them. And if your mate wrongs you, do not keep a record of it, being ready to pull it out and use it against them at an opportune time.

We spent a couple of years remodeling our home. Early one evening Danita and I were sitting in the Jacuzzi, looking up at the freshly installed plastic rain gutters on our house. I had been working hard all day to install them.

"Where is this going to drain?" Danita asked, pointing to the gutter at the roof line of the second story. "Well, they have to drain at this end and that end," I said, pointing to both ends of the house. I went on to explain that I had done everything according to the instructions.

"But I don't want drains all over the place," she said.

"Well, that is what the directions said to do."

Then the clincher came. "I don't want a *Tinker Toy* house!" she said. "Are you calling my work a *Tinker Toy*?!" I exclaimed. "I am constantly working on this house, trying to get it finished. It's got to drain down here. There is nowhere else it can go!"

"Put it around the rocks, over there," she suggested.

We threw ideas back and forth, but it was too late. It was a no-win situation because I was still bothered by her *Tinker Toy* remark. She was not implying my work was clumsy or inept; she simply did not want unsightly plastic drains hanging everywhere. We had two different points of view. The "temperature" in the Jacuzzi suddenly became unbearable, so I got out.

"Why are you getting out now?" she questioned. "I just can't stand being in a Jacuzzi that is too hot," I answered.

But she persisted, "I can tell things are not quite right." We continued our discussion, but nothing got resolved.

I went into the house and started working on a Bible message but could not get anywhere with it. There is never real peace in the home when issues linger and conflict is left unresolved. So I went back outside, gave her a kiss, and asked her if she would like to go for a walk around the neighborhood and see some of the rain gutters on other houses. So we walked around and looked at how some of our neighbors' drains were designed.

While walking and talking, Danita explained, "I didn't mean you did a *Tinker Toy* job. I just don't want plastic hanging everywhere."

I assured her, "It won't. It is going to be really great when I finish." We arrived at a solution, as you will in all conflicts, by coming together and deciding the best plan of action as a couple.

How do you stop a fight? Very simply: When you are wrong, admit it. Sometimes that is very difficult for people. Here are eight little words that open the lines of communication and heal the breach: *"I'm sorry. Please forgive me. I love you."* If you have a limited vocabulary and these words are not found in it, my encouragement to you is to put them at the top of your list. A healthy, happy relationship depends on it.

Whenever you make up following a conflict, remember that you may be completely or partially to blame. It's not wise to minimize your fault in the matter. Remember, the Bible tells us if we stumble in one part of the Law we are guilty of all (James 2:10). If you are 10% wrong in an argument, face the fact that you are 100% wrong in that 10%. Do not point out how much your spouse is to blame. When you "own" your personal failure, before long you will find that your mate will follow your lead and own up to their wrongdoing. Set the example and see what the Lord will do.

In the back of your mind, you may be thinking: *I have said I am sorry. When are they going to say they are sorry?* That is not your problem; it is the Holy Spirit's problem. Take responsibility for your part and let God work on your spouse. If marital conflict only involved you and your mate then the outcome would be doubtful at best. But the Holy Spirit is also part of your relationship. You are responsible to a Higher Authority than the person to whom you are married. Let the Holy Spirit do His work in your marriage.

LET'S DISCUSS HOW TO
FIGHT THE GOOD FIGHT...

1. What types of things do people do willingly while dating that they complain about in marriage?

2. Let's take an honest look at honesty:

   a. Is there such a thing as "good honesty" and "bad honesty"?

   b. Is it ever appropriate to "shade the truth" in a relationship?

3. Can a conflict be resolved without the people actually agreeing? How can the Lord help in that process?

4. Give some examples of how we communicate with body language and tone of voice.

   What messages do they send?

5. Can you think of a time when you witnessed another husband or wife humiliating their mate in front of others?

   How did it make you feel?

6. Give some examples of things that are out of bounds to say to others about one's mate.

7. Are you increasing or decreasing in your critical and/or sarcastic remarks toward each other?

LET'S APPLY WHAT WE'VE LEARNED...

1. What caused the most recent conflict in your marriage?

Did you fight fairly or unfairly? How?

How did you resolve this conflict?

2. Are you excusing dishonesty in your behavior toward your husband/ wife? If so, how?

Will you commit today to be truthful?

3. Take a look at a current conflict in your marriage and work on a solution with your mate.

4. This week, begin to reverse the tendency toward sarcasm, turning instead to praise and encouragement.

CHAPTER FIVE

INTIMACY UNDERMINED

Catch the foxes for us, the little foxes that are ruining the vineyards, while our vineyards are in blossom.
— Song of Solomon 2:15

Romance Under the Table

Once there was a couple who was having difficulty responding to each other, so they went to a marriage counselor. The husband sat on one side of the couch and the wife on the other. Whenever they looked at each other, they glared. The counselor remarked, "I sense that you two are having some real problems."

The couple was stiff, but they managed to talk about their relationship. Finally, the counselor said, "You've got to put some romance back into your marriage. There's got to be more spontaneity. You're too rigid and uptight. This week your homework is to be more romantic, more spontaneous and free-flowing with each other."

The couple came back the following week and this time they sat arm in arm, looking into each other's eyes, star-stricken. It was an absolute reversal. The counselor grinned. "Wow! What did you do? Obviously something exciting has happen in your relationship."

He looked at her and she looked at him; then he said: "Yes, we put the romance and spontaneity back into our relationship. We had a candlelight dinner in a romantic setting. She slid over next to me and we were holding hands, looking deeply into each other's eyes. It was just beautiful. It was so romantic as the candlelight glowed on her face, and I saw a beauty that I remembered back when we were young. Then one thing led to another and it got a bit passionate. We kind of slid under the table."

"You mean ..." the counselor asked, "Right under the table?"

"Yes!"

"Boy, that was spontaneous. Then what happened?"

"Everything was great," they sighed. "But they'll never let us back in that restaurant again!"[14]

Attitudes in Church History

Sex is sometimes difficult to talk about, but as you grow in your relationship with your mate and in the things of the Lord, you will become more comfortable in talking about sexual issues.

Sex used to be a taboo subject in the Church. Prominent figures in Church history, such as Peter Lombardin, Grechien, and others, warned believers that the Holy Spirit left the room when a married couple engaged in sexual intercourse, even if it were for the purpose of procreation. Other Church leaders insisted that God required sexual abstinence during all holy days and seasons. In addition, couples were advised not to have sexual relationships on Thursday, in honor of Christ's arrest; on Friday, in memory of His Crucifixion; on Saturday, in honor of the Virgin Mary; on Sunday, in remembrance of the Resurrection of Christ; and on Monday, out of respect for the departed souls – leaving only Tuesdays and Wednesdays.[15]

If we still had to live according to those Church policies, on Tuesdays and Wednesdays you had both better be in a good mood or else you would end up a very frustrated couple.

The Role of the Wife

The role of both a husband and a wife is a high calling of God. Let us look first at the wife's role in relationship to her husband. Peter gives clear instructions in 1 Peter 3:1-4:

In the same way, you wives, be submissive to your own husbands so that even if any of them are disobedient to the word, they may be won without a word by the behavior of their wives, as they observe your chaste and respectful behavior. Your adornment must not be merely external – braiding the hair, and wearing gold jewelry, or putting on dresses; but let it be the hidden person of the heart, with the imperishable quality of a gentle and quiet spirit, which is precious in the sight of God.

The wife's attention is to be centered on the Lord, letting God work on her inward beauty. She is not to be consumed with the spiritual condition of her husband, but she is to focus on her own relationship with the Lord. However, just because God emphasizes the inward, He is not saying that women should let their outward appearance "go to pot."

The Lord calls the wife to have a gentle and quiet spirit, which means chaste and respectful behavior. Contrary to heeding the instruction of the Lord however, a woman may choose to write her own agenda, and be subtly and persistently manipulative – completely the opposite of what the Lord wants her to be.

Webster's Dictionary defines manipulation as "an unfair and insidious technique that results in getting what one wants." The woman who tends to manipulate decides, "I cannot trust God with my husband. I have to straighten him out on my own." She may try to manipulate him through moodiness, pouting, sulking, scheming, or sexual bargaining. Sometimes she may even turn to lying. A woman who manipulates may get her own way, but she will soon find out that there is no permanent change because she is trusting in her own ability to change and control her husband. Furthermore, not only will she see no permanent change in her mate, but also her manipulation could ruin their relationship. It certainly will not glorify God.

Remember: your husband can be won without a word by your gentle and quiet (peaceable) behavior. Let God do the changing. Trying to change him yourself is a *Mission Impossible*, particularly when it comes to your sexual relationship.

I have counseled couples who have not been intimate with each other for years. I have heard them say, "I can count on one hand the times we have been together in the last year." Sex in marriage is no cure-all, but it is certainly a barometer as to the health of the relationship. In the cases just mentioned, it is a clear signal that something is wrong. It may be that conflicts remain unresolved or that one partner is using sex as a bargaining chip in the relationship. Good fruit will never come out of those kinds of situations.

Take a moment...

Women: Do you employ any manipulative techniques on a regular basis? Are you trusting the Lord for your husband's life? Are you praying or manipulating?

The Role of the Husband

Peter writes to the men, saying: *"Husbands, likewise, dwell with them with understanding, giving honor to the wife, as to the weaker vessel, and as being heirs together of the grace of life, that your prayers may not be hindered. Finally, all of you be of one mind, having compassion for one another; love as brothers, be tenderhearted, be courteous"* (1 Peter 3:7-8 NKJV).

The approach of a husband is much different than the approach of a wife. Men tend to use authority and intimidation to get their way. Especially when a man feels insecure, he resorts to intimidation to get things done. He takes on the role of the Enforcer, imposing his will on the family.

Yet Peter says husbands are to dwell with their wives in an *understanding* way, as with a weaker vessel. The Lord's way – no matter how a man might feel – is to be a servant-leader. The husband is to *understand*, and not *demand* of his wife.

When a man *lords* it over his wife, he is not leading her in the things of the Lord. A wife will either cower or rebel under this type of leadership. Imposed authority bears bad fruit. God's purpose for the sexual part of the marriage will never flourish as long as a husband uses tyranny instead of tenderness to rule the home.

Take a moment...

Men: As a husband, is your approach that of an enforcer or a servant-leader? Does your type of leadership result in genuine respect from your wife?

Cherishing the Weaker Vessel

Peter talks about women being "the weaker vessel." Do not confuse *weaker* with *less valuable*. He is not saying women are less in value.

Let me explain by way of illustration. Coffee cups come in many shapes and sizes. You might have your own favorite style. Certain ceramic mugs are thick and clumsy – so heavy you almost need both hands to lift them. Then there are also thin, delicate, fine china cups that are dainty and petite. Both serve their intended purpose for drinking coffee or tea. But if you took the ceramic mug and the fine china and clanged them together, which do you think would shatter? Certainly, the weaker, more delicate china cup would. So too, when you clash with your wife, you can easily hurt her feelings and break her spirit.

When God declares the woman to be the weaker vessel, He is simply making a distinction between how He created the different sexes. In our "politically correct" society, we want to deny that fact, but we do so to our own peril.

Women are created differently than men. A woman has a refined sense of her surroundings. She is very sensitive to what goes on around her. Her emotions are finely tuned. Men are not that way. They are more like the clumsy coffee mug. Things that touch the emotions of a woman do not as easily touch the emotions of a man. What may hurt a woman may not necessarily affect a man. Therefore, men need to be careful when a clash takes place in the home, for they have the power to *shatter* or *shelter* their wives.

It is important for men to learn that God created the woman in such a way that she responds when treated with kindness, gentleness, and sensitivity to her feelings and needs. Wives will not respond to commands and demands, but will readily respond when the husband is understanding. This is why Peter instructs men not to use a heavy hand in dealing with their wives.

Take a moment...

How important is your sexual relationship with your husband/wife? Are regular times of physical intimacy important to you?

Pornography:
Its Ill Effects in the Bedroom

The man that tries to use intimidation to get what he wants in the bedroom is in for a rude awakening. Some men make unreasonable and unwise demands upon their wives when it comes to the sexual part of their relationship. In counseling situations, men have confessed to wanting their wives to participate in the strange sexual fantasies that they picked up in their youth, even to the point of involving pornography.

A man whose marriage I had officiated once asked me: "Is it okay if we look at pornographic videos in our sexual relationship?" My response was, "Go ahead – if you want to destroy your wife. It may stimulate you, but it will ruin her. You will not build trust and intimacy that way." Our pre-marital sessions had not covered pornography, so this really surprised me. I would not have married them and put the woman into such jeopardy if I had known the quirkiness of this fellow.

When a man begins to ask his wife to involve herself in his strange sexual fantasies, she will feel cheap and used.

Her value as a woman and wife will suffer as she becomes a sexual tool and the facilitator of her husband's salacious imaginations. Once this starts, it is very difficult to stop. Like a train going down the tracks at 100 mph, it takes awhile to slow down; you cannot stop quickly.

A man who involves himself in pornography will find it very difficult to form and cultivate a meaningful and deep relationship with his wife. Romance will be replaced with fantasy and raw passion. He will have a hard time expressing sensitivity and tenderness toward her as deep satisfaction and true intimacy in the relationship becomes more and more elusive.

God has made us body, soul, and spirit. Before we were born again of the Spirit of God, we were controlled by our bodily appetites. Now there has been a reversal. The spirit is uppermost and God wants to direct our lives by His Holy Spirit.

As Christians, we are complete in Christ. We are spirit, soul, and body integrated into a new creation. The Bible says that old things have passed away and new things have come (2 Corinthians 5:17). True satisfaction will never come from that which is old and artificial. That includes the sexual part of our being.

When God is the center of a marriage, the result is deeper intimacy. God also heals any damage done by time misspent in promiscuity prior to our coming to faith in Christ. Remember: God created sex. Once we are in Christ, no *Playboy* or *Playgirl* philosophy can compete with God's genuine article.

Take a moment...

Does your intimate behavior show dignity and honor to your mate?

Does it show that you value them?

Principles for Intimacy in Marriage

Adhering to biblical principles will foster intimacy in a marriage. The principles are meant to correct misconceptions and to undo the worldly patterns that take away from intimacy instead of adding to it. These guidelines are applicable both to couples that began their relationship *in the Lord* and to those that did not know Christ when they first met.

Danita and I dated for about three years before we were married, and during that time, we did not live to please God. When we did finally marry, we had undermined the moral foundation of our relationship. After we were saved, we realized God's ideal for intimacy and looked to Him for guidance in this area. What follows is a blueprint for intimacy.

1. Hold a Godly View of Sexuality

We need to have the proper attitude regarding sexuality. You may need to reprogram an XXX-rated mindset about sex and change it to a godly concept. After all, who knows more about sex than God Himself? He created it. If you bought a new car and six months later, you started having trouble with it, you would not go to the junkyard for service. You would go back to the dealer. So too, when a person has a pornographic bent toward sexuality, they are shopping in a sexual junkyard. They need to return to the dealer – God Himself.

Some people cringe when they hear the words *God* and *sex* in the same sentence. The enemy would like to keep it that way. Typically, all we ever hear about sex comes from the media or from those who promote a less-than-godly idea of sexuality. They use sex for their own agendas, promoting promiscuity or pornography in the name of sexual freedom. As a result, even Christians do not always have healthy ideas about sex and marriage: they either have a worldly view of human sexuality or consider it taboo. Unfortunately, we rarely hear a healthy balance between the two.

God desires married couples to take joy and pleasure in the sexual experience. A healthy perspective of the physical relationship between husband and wife is extremely important in order for a couple to discover all that God has for them.

When building a home, you must first have a good set of blueprints; and you do not start interior decorating before laying the foundation. So it is with marriage. The sexual part is like interior design: it comes *after* the foundation is poured and set. The joy to be experienced in the bedroom is a result of what fills your head beforehand: God's foundation.

The Bible tells us that we were made in the image and likeness of God. That means He created us with dignity and value. He also created us to have sexual desires and a deep capacity for intimacy. But along with this, God has given us the context in which our sexual desires are to be fulfilled. When we try to find sexual satisfaction outside of this God-given context, we end up frustrated, unfulfilled, and overcome by the *Solomon-syndrome.*

King Solomon had seven hundred wives and three hundred concubines (that is one thousand intimate relationships), and he still wasn't satisfied! Why? He took sex out of the context in which God had established it – and in which he himself had once found satisfaction, judging by his confession in *Song of Solomon.*

In Acts 10, the Apostle Peter was given a vision of a great sheet coming down from Heaven, which was lowered by its four corners to the ground. In it were all kinds of four-footed animals, crawling creatures of the earth, and birds of the air. The Lord called to him, *"Kill and eat!"* But Peter said, *"Not so Lord, I have never eaten anything unclean."* The Lord then declared, "Do not call unclean that which I have cleansed." God was saying all foods were now kosher, and in a broader sense, the separation between Jew and Gentile was ended.

Let me broaden it a bit more. You may have come out of a background where sex was a big hang-up in your life, so much so that any association with intimacy creates thoughts of a sinful past and feelings of immorality and dirtiness. You cannot turn your brain off when these thoughts fill your mind, but realize this: you are a new creation in Christ and so is the sexual part of your being. So "what God has cleansed, no longer call unclean."

I remember a couple that had lived very promiscuous lives before coming to Christ. They were saved as singles, then later met and got married as Christians. In counseling, they told me, "We cannot enjoy our sexual relationship because we have all these thoughts in our minds about previous partners." Impure fantasies from past relationships were ruining what God had for them now in their relationship as a Christian husband and wife. It took time to work out what had been fed into their minds, but God is able *"by the washing of regeneration and renewing by the Holy Spirit"* (Titus 3:5) to renew the mind. After twenty years, they are doing great, raising their children in ministry, and maintaining a happy marriage.

2. Allow Sex to Be Pleasurable

The Bible talks openly about sexual pleasure in marriage. In fact, I often suggest couples read the book *Solomon on Sex* by Joseph Dillow. It goes through Song of Solomon, dealing with many aspects of Solomon's love life with the Shulamite woman.

The Bible tells us in Proverbs 5:15, *"Drink water from your own cistern, and fresh water from your own well."* The writer is talking about the sexual experience. Go to your own cistern – your own wife or husband – and be refreshed. Proverbs 5:19 says, *"Let her breasts satisfy you at all times."* Literally, it means to permit satisfaction. You have to fix in your mind that your spouse is the only one you are going to permit to satisfy you sexually.

In the fifth chapter of Song of Solomon, the author describes the love of a woman for her husband and the pleasure she experiences with him. The woman verbalizes her feelings and we should take note of how important that is in the marital relationship.

The woman says:

My lover is dark and dazzling,
*   better than ten thousand others!*
His head is finest gold,
*   his wavy hair is black as a raven.*
His eyes sparkle like doves
*   beside springs of water;*
They are set like jewels
*   washed in milk.*

His cheeks are like gardens of spices
    giving off fragrance.
His lips are like lilies,
    perfumed with myrrh.
His arms are like rounded bars of gold,
    set with beryl.
His body is like bright ivory,
    glowing with lapis lazuli.
His legs are like marble pillars
    set in sockets of finest gold.
His posture is stately,
    like the noble cedars of Lebanon.

                        – Song of Solomon 5:10-15 NLT

Likewise, Solomon describes his beautiful bride in chapter seven:

How beautiful are your sandaled feet,
    O queenly maiden.
Your rounded thighs are like jewels,
    the work of a skilled craftsman.
Your navel is perfectly formed
    like a goblet filled with mixed wine.
Between your thighs lies a mound of wheat
    bordered with lilies.
Your breasts are like two fawns,
    twin fawns of a gazelle.
Your neck is as beautiful as an ivory tower.
Your eyes are like the sparkling pools in Heshbon
    by the gate of Bath-rabbim.
Your nose is as fine as the tower of Lebanon
    overlooking Damascus.
Your head is as majestic as Mount Carmel,
    and the sheen of your hair radiates royalty.
The king is held captive by its tresses.

Oh, how beautiful you are!
  How pleasing, my love, how full of delights!
You are slender like a palm tree,
  and your breasts are like its clusters of fruit.
I said, "I will climb the palm tree
  and take hold of its fruit."
May your breasts be like grape clusters,
  and the fragrance of your breath like apples.
May your kisses be as exciting as the best wine,
  flowing gently over lips and teeth.
                              – Song of Solomon 7:1-9 NLT

This probably is not how we would describe our mates today. Solomon and the Shulamite used poetic language and figures of speech common to their day to describe each other. This is typical in Scripture.

We see the same use of figurative language in the New Testament. During the time the Apostle Paul spent in a Philippian prison chained to a Roman guard, he developed those illustrations he used in Ephesians 6 to describe the full armor of God. He pictured the everyday armor of a Roman soldier, and likened it to our spiritual armament: the helmet of salvation, the breastplate of righteousness, and so on. Similarly, the poetry in Song of Solomon uses common objects of the day to describe the romance between a man and his wife, transforming the ordinary into a thing of beauty.

Proverbs 5:18-20 says, *"Let your fountain be blessed, and rejoice in the wife of your youth. As a loving hind and a graceful doe, let her breasts satisfy you at all times; be exhilarated always with her love. For why should you, my son, be exhilarated with an adulteress, and embrace the bosom of a foreigner?"* Here Solomon is confessing the fact that adultery will never satisfy a person. Those who commit it once are prone to repeat it. They simply move from one adulterous relationship to another. And keep in mind, *30 minutes* of unchecked passion can lead to *30 years* of pain and regret.

You must make a conscious choice to permit your mate to satisfy you. Husbands and wives are like a lock and key: one is no good without the other.

In considering spiritual warfare in marriage, we need to understand that the strategy of Satan is to gain a foothold in our relationships. One way he does it is to convince you that your marriage is boring and stale, that your mate is not the special person you once thought they were. Giving in to these suggestions is to make common what God has made unique, and a sense of dissatisfaction and discontent will inevitably follow.

Whenever a person grows dissatisfied with their mate, the root of the problem is actually dissatisfaction with God. It is a denial of the plan of God and His work in your marriage. You lose sight of the fact that God is perfecting your marriage and maturing your partner in their role as husband or wife. Therefore, be vigilant and watch for the subtle ways in which the enemy works. *"Resist the devil and he will flee from you"* (James 4:7).

Take a moment...

Have you considered it a goal to keep your mate sexually satisfied, or have you only been concerned with your own satisfaction?

3. Keep Sex within Your Marriage

Sex is to be practiced within marriage, not outside of it or before the wedding takes place. Doing so brings guilt, shame, and a dulled sensitivity to your mate, no matter how liberated society says you are to be. If a couple engages in sex before marriage, the woman will feel like she was not worth the wait. She will feel betrayed by the one who is supposed to be the head and protector of the home.

Often, in these cases, after the couple marries, the wife tends to dominate the home. Why? Because the trust factor is broken. God made her to *respond* to her husband. If the man proved untrustworthy during the courtship by initiating sex, she will find it very difficult to trust her home and well-being to him after they are married. Her natural reflex is to look out for herself, and so she will take on a more aggressive role. The cycle can only be broken over time as the husband leads the family in the ways of the Lord.

Typically, I have seen husbands respond to a dominating wife by retreating into passivity. If the man has created this scenario by being a poor spiritual role model, he needs to take the initiative and break the pattern.

A wife will take charge if necessary. She may not feel comfortable in this role but, like Zipporah who filled the gap when her husband Moses flaked out (Exodus 4:24-26), she will do it to preserve her family. The more aggressive the wife becomes, the less assertive the husband tends to be, and it turns into a vicious cycle. This imbalance can at times be traced back to misplaced intimacy – sex before marriage.

Rain and sunshine cause a healthy tree to grow, but these same elements can also create wood rot. Likewise, when sex is taken outside of God's context of marriage, it can rot a relationship and make people bitter. *If you want the honeymoon to never end, practice biblical sex.*

4. Make It Right

What do you do if you have already engaged in sex before marriage? Remember God is redemptive: He takes the worst of situations and turns them around. It is no different in your case.

First of all, acknowledge that you have sinned against God and His ideal plan for marriage. He is your Creator and has given you certain capacities. The sex drive is one. He ordained precise parameters in which this part of your life is to be practiced; it is designed only for after you are married. If you have gone outside of God's design for sex, you are guilty. Confess what you have done to God and He will forgive you. First John 1:9 tells us, *"If we confess our sins, He is faithful and righteous to forgive us our sins and to cleanse us from all unrighteousness."*

Second, you need to realize that you have sinned against your mate. You may protest, "It was consensual. She was just as willing as I was!" That may be true, but it does not lessen your responsibility to go to your mate and ask forgiveness for violating a fundamental precept of marriage.

Here is a prayer that might help as you go before God and your mate:

"Father, I am sorry that I have fallen short of Your perfect plan for my marriage. I have sinned and I take full responsibility."

Next, verbalize it to each other:

"Honey, I am sorry that I did not put God first in our relationship. Forgive me for taking advantage of

the situation and not controlling my passions. I have sinned against God and against you."

"I'm sorry. I love you. Please forgive me."

Once you do that, you have a brand new start. Now you can look forward to the great things God has for you.

When you cover your sin on the other hand, it becomes a festering sore that can destroy your relationship. Proverbs 28:13 says, *"He who covers his sins will not prosper, but whoever confesses and forsakes them will have mercy"* (NKJV). God has great things planned for your marriage. Simply let Him have His way.

5. Be Unselfish in Your Affections

Our affections are not to be primarily for self-gratification, but we are to be committed to the satisfaction of our spouse. It is quite natural to seek our own fulfillment, however it is not biblical to stop there. God has designed us so that full sexual satisfaction will only be met when mutual fulfillment is achieved. The Bible says in 1 Corinthians 7:3, *"The husband must fulfill his duty to his wife, and likewise also the wife to her husband."* The passage speaks of not only pleasing ourselves but also seeking to please our mate in the sexual experience.

6. Do Not Deprive Your Mate

Since God has given each of us a sex drive to be used within the proper context of marriage, we must not deny our mate. *"Stop depriving one another, except by agreement ... and come together again"* (1 Corinthians 7:5).

Sex should never be used as a tool to get even with your spouse or to get your own way. If a person loses interest in the sexual part of marriage – that which God has made to be such a natural part of the relationship – it signals a deeper problem.

If you both agree to abstain from sexual activity for spiritual or physical reasons, as our passage states, it is to be short term. For example, you may agree to abstain in order to pray and fast together. It appears this is what Paul is indicating. But if your sexual relationship has been *put on hold* for an extended period of time, something is wrong. It is not natural for a couple to do this and the enemy will use it to lead one or both into temptation.

Gender and Sex

What does sexuality mean to a woman? It is critical to the self-acceptance of a wife that her husband be satisfied with her as his sexual partner. She thinks, "Do I satisfy him? Is he taking pleasure in my body and in me as a sexual partner?" If she does not feel that way, problems will arise in the relationship.

The brain is the control center of a woman for love-making. Here are three areas that affect her.

1: What She Thinks about Sex

Does she have a healthy attitude about sexuality? I knew a certain woman that grew up with a "say no to sex" mantra drilled into her mind all her life, so she was not prepared for her honeymoon. She found that she could not bring herself to "say yes" even when it was appropriate to do so as a bride.

2: What She Thinks about Herself

Does the woman have a self-deprecating image? Does she belittle herself, or think very lowly of herself? Or does she have a proper self-image, understanding that she is "fearfully and wonderfully made, and wonderful are the works of God" (see Psalm 139:14)?

A poor self-image will greatly affect a women's view of her sexuality and desirability to her husband.

3: What She Thinks about Her Husband

This is very important area for a woman. If she has a lowly view of her husband, things will not go well in the bedroom. When a woman has a critical attitude toward her husband, it will show up in their sexual relationship. The satisfaction God intended will be elusive.

Philippians 4:8 instructs us: *"Whatever is true, whatever is honorable, whatever is right, whatever is pure, whatever is lovely, whatever is of good repute, if there is any excellence and if anything worthy of praise, [let your mind] dwell on these things."* Love grows as our thought patterns change from negative to positive.

What do you think about your husband? Concentrate on those things he does well and pray about the things that irritate you. If your love relationship has become stale, evaluate what thoughts you are entertaining about your mate and make the appropriate changes. Try praise instead of put-downs. When we think differently, we act differently, and the sexual relationship will be greatly affected.

Sex is never to be used as a tool or a bargaining chip. The marriage bed should never be used as an arena to get what you want or to punish your mate. You belong to the Lord and it is His will to reign and rule in your home. There should be no place where one mate seeks to exert control over the other. The only controlling force in the home is to be the Holy Spirit.

Have you wholly given your husband or wife over to the care and control of the Lord? Or are you still seeking to change them yourself? Is it *"Thy will be done"* in their lives or is it *your* will be done?

The enemy says, "Live for yourself. Take control. Get in there and change things." He used this same lie with Eve in the Garden of Eden, and he will use it with you today if you let him. But God says, "Trust Me. I will never leave or forsake you" (see Hebrews 13:5); and "I am at work in you to will and do My good pleasure" (see Philippians 2:13).

When we stop believing the lies of Satan about marriage and let the power of God's forgiveness and love flow through our lives, then the supernatural begins to happen. Allow God "to do exceeding abundantly above all you ask or think" (see Ephesians 3:20).

The Effect of Pornography on Intimacy

For the man, sexual arousal is triggered by sight. He is not as concerned about what his mate is thinking or feeling. His engine gets started just by looking. While his wife thinks of the sexual relationship as an emotional experience, the man is quite different. She could be undressing for the sole purpose of getting into bed to go to sleep – or intending just to read for a while – but as he is watching her, he gets sexually excited. He thinks, "She's doing this because she wants me." It is a total misunderstanding on his part.

Yet although men are stimulated by sight, pornography will kill your desire for your mate. Why? God has created us for relationships, and in pornography, there is no relationship. You cannot have intimacy with a celluloid image or dots of ink on the page of a magazine. It is totally unreal and completely self-absorbing. It replaces reality with fantasy.

As a married man, God has given you a real woman with whom you can have a sexual relationship. If pornography has been a fetish, get rid of it and begin the process of flushing your mind of its images and replacing them with the Word of God and with the love of a real person: your wife.

Disneyland is famous for fantasy. After a day spent there you might say, "Wow, that was a lot of fun! Wouldn't it be great to live there?! Everything is magical and wonderful. There are cartoon characters walking around, light shows at night, and music filling the air. I don't want to live in the *real* world anymore; I am going to live at Disneyland." The problem is, it's just fantasy, unreal and imaginary. Besides, you eventually would be asked to leave. You cannot live there; you have to go back into the real world.

It is the same with sexual fantasies and pornography. You can't *live* there. And if you try, it will destroy you and your relationship with your mate. That's why the Bible says, *"Rejoice in the wife of your youth ... be exhilarated always with her love"* (Proverbs 5:18-19). Pornography is a bottomless pit of perversion that will suck the life out of your marriage.

Sexual addiction to pornography can be as powerful as addiction to heroin. The greater the propensity to continue in that lifestyle, the greater the effort needed to break it's patterns.

A fellow in our church began a class called "The Most Excellent Way," which primarily addresses drug and alcohol addiction, but can be adapted to deal with sexual addiction as well. It is important to go to whatever lengths necessary to kick the pornography habit. Accountability in a men's group or pastoral counseling is often needed.

Any type of relationship that would threaten the well-being of the marriage, especially when it touches areas dealing with personal intimacy, must be cut off completely.

Jesus had some strong words in Matthew 18:8-9, describing the severity with which we must deal with besetting sins:

If your hand or your foot causes you to stumble, cut it off and throw it from you; it is better for you to enter life crippled or lame, than to have two hands or two feet and be cast into the eternal fire. If your eye causes you to stumble, pluck it out and throw it from you. It is better for you to enter life with one eye, than to have two eyes and be cast into the fiery hell.

Cut it off and cast it away. It might be an inappropriate relationship at work or with a friend or neighbor; it might be an on-line relationship; it might be provocative computer images you're constantly viewing. Anyone or anything that arouses passion other than your spouse must be cut off, otherwise longterm marital satisfaction will suffer.

In the final analysis, your relationship with Jesus is at the core of a happy marriage. You began in the Spirit when you received Christ as your Savior. Now continue in the Spirit. Whether it concerns sexuality or any other important issue in marriage, you can either give control of it over to the Lord or struggle with it unsuccessfully in your flesh.

Take a moment...

Does your mate have access to your computer? Would they be surprised at what they would find if they checked your history, emails, etc? Do you need to be more "technologically accountable"?

LET'S DISCUSS
INTIMACY UNDERMINED...

1. Peter extols the virtues of a woman who has *"the imperishable quality of a gentle and quiet spirit."* What does that mean?

   How might that be different from being a gentle and quiet person?

2. How does having a "servant's heart" break the cycle of an overly-demanding spirit?

3. What are some ways to build closeness and connection in a marriage?

   How can you counteract the enemy's attempts to make you feel discontented with your marriage?

4. What safeguards can couples implement to protect themselves against the temptation that comes via the Internet?

Let's Apply What We've Learned...

1. Have you allowed negative thoughts about your mate to affect your marriage?

   You can take those thoughts captive right now and renew your relationship. Choose God's perspective.

2. Are you taking real steps to safeguard your sexual purity?

   a. Do you need to confess anything to God and your mate – whether it happened before or during your marriage?

   b. Has anything undermined the moral foundation of your marriage? Take time to get together with your mate and deal with it right now.

   c. Are you hiding pornography or sexual imagery from your spouse? Get rid of it, before it destroys your marriage.

   d. Are there any things, people, behaviors, etc. that you need to eliminate from your life in order to keep your marital intimacy from being undermined?

3. Do you worship the Lord in your marital intimacy?

    Pray together this week before or after those intimate times with your mate, and be specific about those areas in which you need God's touch and His healing.

Chapter Six

Battle-Plan Prayer

*We can do much after we pray; but until we pray, we
cannot do anything but pray.*

If you were leaving hurriedly on a trip and had to call home
and give instructions for maintaining the household, what
would be Number One on your list? What would be your
priority? Feeding the dog? Locking the doors? Watering the
plants? Letting the cat out? Getting the mail? What would
be first on the list?

In the book of 1 Timothy, the Apostle Paul is writing to
his young co-worker, whom he had sent to Ephesus to pastor
the church there. Paul is telling Timothy how believers are
to conduct themselves in the household of God. In essence,
he is "calling" back home to say: This is a priority in the
household of God; this is the number one item to which we
should give ourselves as believers in our individual lives,
in our marriages, and in the Church. Paul says, *"First of
all, then, I urge that entreaties and prayers, petitions and
thanksgivings, be made on behalf of all men, for kings and
all who are in authority, so that we may lead a tranquil and
quiet life in all godliness and dignity"* (1 Timothy 2:1-2).

The word "urge" is so important; it speaks to all of us.
You need to feel the passion Paul put into that statement.
It is as if he were to come up, put his arm around you, and
draw you close to himself. That is what the term means: "to
call to one's side; to advise or admonish." Picture a coach

pulling players aside in a critical game to instruct and exhort them, laying out the strategy for the winning play. "Come here, you are an important part of this team and we want to win the game. Here is the strategy ..." That is what it means to "urge."

It is not a picture of us sitting on the bench twiddling our thumbs and looking off into space. We want to feel Paul's passion and desire so that a difference might take place in our marriage and for the kingdom of God. He is saying, "Before you do anything else, pray."

Take a moment...

Are you using prayer as part of your strategy for having a healthy marriage?

There are four distinct parts to prayer in this passage, like different rooms in the same house. Matthew Henry sums up the four parts of Paul's prayer in this way: entreaties, for the averting of evil; *prayers*, for the obtaining of good; *petitions*, for others; and *thanksgivings*, for mercies already received.[16]

We are going to look at them one at a time, but keep in mind it is not always easy to delineate between them; sometimes they overlap one another. It is not really critical to know which one we are praying, otherwise our prayers could become sterile and mechanical. The idea is to bring our lives and marriages (along with these general principles) before God that we might pray with power. The Holy Spirit will guide the direction, scope, and content of our prayers.

We need to be open to Him because it is by His power that we can use these tools.

1: Entreaties

The first type of prayer is the *entreaty*. The idea of the word entreaty is "prayer for favor in some special need."[17] A particular circumstance has arisen in your life, so you entreat the Lord concerning it.

One purpose for entreaties is for the *averting of evil*. Maybe there is a critical situation pending, like a court case, a doctor's report, or marital separation. Entreaties are made to the Lord to avert evil and grant mercy. We feel a sense of need but at the same time a lack of ability to meet that need, so we entreat the Lord.

When I first became a Christian, my wife Danita wanted nothing to do with me or with Jesus, and divorce was imminent. Much entreaty went up to the Lord to avert that evil.

This same word is used with Zacharias and Elizabeth in Luke 1. Remember the two of them? Their son was John the Baptist, the cousin of Jesus. The Bible says Zacharias and Elizabeth were both righteous, both blameless according to the Law of God, yet Elizabeth was barren. They were also old; it did not look like there was much hope for having a family.

It is a difficult thing for a couple not to be able to have children. It troubles their hearts and unsettles their minds, and has the potential of dividing them. Spiritually there was nothing wrong with Zacharias and Elizabeth. God was not withholding from them because they were backslidden. They were good people, but we find that there are times when God does not act immediately, even for good people.

The Bible says in the first chapter of the Gospel of Luke that Zacharias was doing his priestly service – ministering in the Temple on behalf of others – and he was no doubt also offering up prayers for Elizabeth and himself. Perhaps he prayed something like: "O God, have mercy on my wife. It is so important to her to have a child. It matters to me too, but it is especially breaking her heart." He offered entreaties to God because he in himself was powerless to do anything about the situation. And the Bible says in Luke 1:13: *"The angel said to him, 'Do not be afraid, Zacharias, for your petition* [or your entreaty] *has been heard, and your wife Elizabeth will bear you a son, and you will give him the name John.'"*

There is another place in Scripture where the word *entreaty* is used. It was when Jesus Christ was in the Garden of Gethsemane. He was sweating great drops of blood because of the stress He endured. Three times He prayed, *"Father, if it is possible, let this cup pass from Me; yet not as I will, but as You will"* (Matthew 26:39). That prayer was an entreaty.

Even Jesus expressed human need. He did not depend upon His divine nature. He experienced what we experience: He depended upon the Father by way of the use of entreaties. *"In the days of His flesh, He offered up both prayers and supplications with loud crying and tears to the One able to save Him from death, and He was heard because of His piety"* (Hebrews 5:7). Notice, Jesus was heard, yet He went to the Cross. He was heard by the One who was able to deliver Him. And how did God deliver Him? He delivered Him to the Cross because that was the will of God the Father.

My entreaties to God for my wife's conversion and for my children's well-being were radical and fanatical. Many late nights I prayed in the living room or out in the backyard under the stars. I was a young Christian and very zealous for God's will to be done in our home. I realized how I had brought evil into the home over the years, and I was literally *desperate in prayer.*

My prayers at the time were not the "Now I lay me down to sleep" type. These prayers were very impassioned and much time was spent in rebuking the Devil, whose presence I thought I had brought into our home. The prayers went something like this:

"O, God, please help! Forgive me of the horrible mess I have made of things! Please save my wife. Please protect my kids."

"I rebuke you, Satan, in Jesus' name. Your place is in the lake of fire that burns forever and ever. Be gone from this household; you have no power or authority here."

"Jesus, fill this house with Your presence."

Since the drugs, false religion, and perverse lifestyle that were part of my life for seven years of marriage were now bearing evil fruit and clashing with my new-found faith, I could sense the spiritual warfare going on in our home. It all came down to the question of which power was going to win. Through these entreaties to the Lord – impassioned, radical, and fanatical – God destroyed the Devil's stronghold in our home. The Lord brought my wife to a saving knowledge of Christ, and as our children grew, they all made their own decisions to follow the Lord.

2: Prayers

Another type of communication with God is simply called *prayers.* This word in the Greek is a term that means, "getting things we need."[18] It is not bad to pray for things that we need personally or as a couple, whether they are spiritual or material things. It is a means of devotion.

Once again, Jesus is the model for us. When He was about to choose His twelve apostles, He didn't say, "Eenie, meenie, minie, moe ..." He did not even use the keen discernment that comes when you are God the Son. And He did not look at the outward appearance of the men. Instead, the Bible tells us in Luke 6:12-13: *"He went off to the mountain to pray, and He spent the whole night in prayer to God. And when day came, He called His disciples to Him and chose twelve of them, whom He also named as apostles."* He spent all night in prayer before He chose these men.

We often do things differently than the Lord; we respond more like the prophet Samuel. In 1 Samuel 16, God told the prophet to go to the house of Jesse because He was going to choose a king to replace Saul. Samuel said to Jesse, "Let me see your sons." So Jesse brought out his boys. First was the eldest, Eliab, and Samuel thought, "Surely this is God's man." Why did he say that? He said it because Eliab was a strong, handsome man, head and shoulders above everyone else. But God said, "No. He is not the one I have chosen." This happened with seven of Jesse's sons, but none of them were God's choice. "Do you have any other sons?" Samuel asked. "There is David, the youngest," implying he is the *least*, not even worthy of consideration. David was passed over by his father and brothers, but he was God's choice. Man looks at the *outward appearance* but God looks at the *heart.*

We are prone to look at a person and think, "They have an attractive appearance. God could really use them. Look how smart and industrious they are. We need someone who has good looks, is intelligent, and oh, an added bonus – they are very witty. And they have money. Bring them on board."

We look at the outward instead of doing what Jesus did: He prayed over decisions. Often those that the world passes over are the ones God chooses. This is such an important principle in choosing the mate that God has for you. Do not make your choice primarily because he or she looks good to you, or you may find yourself waking up to the truth that *beauty is only skin deep.*

The first century church made prayer a priority. It was a key element. Acts 2:42 says, *"They were continually devoting themselves to the apostles' teaching and to fellowship, to the breaking of bread and to prayer."* Married couples need to pray together. Pray together in the morning, pray on the way to work, pray on the way to church, pray at meal times, pray at night, pray alone and together – we need to pray all the time. Prayer moves the hand of God in our lives, our marriages and families, and in the Church.

I believe we are not seeing more of the supernatural in the Church and in marriages today because we lack prayer. If we would simply pray, God would meet us and do greater works in and though us. "We can do much after we pray, but until we pray, we cannot do anything but pray."

Take a moment...

How would you describe your prayer life? Circle the term that fits best: Almost Non-existent / Crisis Only / Lukewarm / Needs Improvement / Consistent

It was a rainy Thursday afternoon over 130 summers ago, and a pile of sworn statements and legal documents say this story is true:

There was just one problem with Swan Quarter, North Carolina. It was lowland. So naturally, the choicest real estate was on the highest ground. In the event of heavy rains the closer you were to sea level the harder you were hit.

The Methodists of Swan Quarter had no church and the only lot available on which to build was a plot of low-lying property on Oyster Creek Road. It was far from an ideal location, but they acquired the land, and the construction began. The church was to be a white frame, small but sturdy, propped up on brick pilings. In 1876 the building was completed, and on Sunday, September 16, a rousing dedication service was celebrated.

Three days later, on Wednesday, a terrible storm hit Swan Quarter. All day the winds howled and the rain came down in a gray wall of water. Nightfall brought devastation. Much of the town was flooded; many roofs were ripped from homes by the hurricane-force winds. The storm raged on all through the night and into the bleak morning. By Thursday afternoon, the winds subsided and the rain all but stopped.

For the first time in more than a day, there was an eerie calm. One by one the citizens of Swan Quarter folded back their shutters and peered from what was left of their homes. Most saw only a desolate waterscape, a community ravaged by nature. But those within sight of Oyster Creek Road saw the most incredible sight they had ever seen. The Swan Quarter Methodist Church – the whole building intact – was floating down the street!

The floodwater had gently lifted the entire structure from the brick pilings on which it had rested and sent it off, slowly, silently, down Oyster Creek Road. Within minutes, several concerned townsfolk were sloshing about in the street, waist deep, fighting the rushing current, trying desperately to reach the still-moving church so that they could moor it with lengths of rope. The ropes were fastened, but the effort was useless. There was no stable structure secure enough to restrain the floating chapel.

As the building passed by, more attention was drawn and more aid was enlisted, but to no avail. The church moved on. By now the building had made its way to the center of town, still on Oyster Creek Road. Then as dozens of amazed, helpless citizens watched, the Swan Quarter Methodist Church, still floating, made a sharp inexplicable right turn and continued down another road, as if the chapel itself were alive or had a mind of its own. For two more blocks, the townsfolk fought with ropes to hold it back but all in vain. And then, in the same decisive manner with which it had moved, the church veered off the road, headed for the center of a vacant lot and there stopped.

When the flood water receded, the church remained, and it is there to this day. The prime highland lot where the chapel settled was the first choice, the ideal parcel for the Methodist Church. They had made an offer and diligently prayed but it seemed to no avail. The shrewd, wealthy landowner whose property it originally was turned them down flat. The morning after the flood, after discovering the church in the middle of his lot, that same landowner went straight to the Methodist minister and with trembling hands presented him with the deed to the property.[19]

Certainly, in this case, we see that *"the effective, fervent prayer of a righteous man avails much"* (James 5:16 NKJV). Know that prayer can do the miraculous in your relationship as well. God can move your marriage from a place of ordeal to one of ideal.

3: Petitions

The third type of prayer is called *petition* or *intercession*. This is "a pleading for others."

I do not always know how to pray as I ought, but the Holy Spirit does. Jesus knows my need before I ask and so He is there before the throne of God interceding. Romans 8:26-27 says, *"In the same way the Spirit also helps our weakness; for we do not know how to pray as we should, but the Spirit Himself intercedes for us with groanings too deep for words; and He who searches the hearts knows what the mind of the Spirit is, because He intercedes for the saints according to the will of God."* The Spirit intercedes for us when we do not know how to pray. Romans 8:34 tells us, *"Who is the one who condemns? Christ Jesus is He who died, yes, rather who was raised, who is at the right hand of God, who also intercedes for us."* So not only does Jesus intercede for us, but the Spirit does as well.

Prayer is offered on our behalf as soon as we bring our hearts before the throne of God and say, "Lord, go before me. Intercede in this situation. I do not know how to pray for this situation, Lord, but You do. You know the end from the beginning, so now intercede, plead my case for me."

I spent many a night in this kind of prayer when my own marriage looked hopeless. Danita and I were at odds with each other and things seemed as if they would never change. But they did.

Many times you will not know how to pray for your mate, and they, in turn, will not know how to pray for you. So pray, "Lord, deal with them, bless them, or touch them in the way they need to be touched. You know what they need, Lord. Please move in their life." The Bible says, *"Therefore He is able also to save forever those who draw near to God through Him, since He [Jesus] always lives to make intercession for them"* (Hebrews 7:25). Notice the on-going intercession on our behalf done by Jesus Himself and the Holy Spirit.

You find that most couples will pray at meals, and the meal is blessed by that petition. Where did we get that habit? Our practice came from 1 Timothy 4:4-5: *"For everything created by God is good, and nothing is to be rejected if it is received with gratitude; for it is sanctified by means of the word of God and prayer."*

James tells us, *"Therefore, confess your sins to one another, and pray for one another so that you may be healed. The effective prayer of a righteous man can accomplish much"* (James 5:16). The Bible exhorts us to make petitions for one another – this practice is especially beneficial in bringing blessings upon our marriages.

4: Thanksgivings

The last type of prayer, the fourth room in the house, is *thanksgiving.* The Greek term for the word thanksgiving is *eucharistia.*[20] from which we get our English word "Eucharist." It carries the idea of giving "gratitude to God as an act of worship."[21] It is declaring thanks and praise unto God.

A lack of believing God for answered prayer is directly related to a lack in responding to God with thanksgiving. In Luke 17, we read that Jesus healed 10 lepers, but only one of them took the time to come back and thank Him.

I call those others the "Thankless Nine." We need to be careful we are not like them.

R.A. Torrey, in his classic book *How to Pray,* exhorts believers concerning the connection between thankfulness for what God has done in the past, and their ability to believe Him for what He wants to do right now. When we neglect to give thanks to God for answered prayers in the past, we diminish our faith and the power for believing God to answer our prayers in the future.

The Bible says, *"In everything give thanks; for this is God's will for you in Christ Jesus"* (1 Thessalonians 5:18). It is important to develop a habitual attitude of thanksgiving. As you look back over all that God has done for you, start to meditate on those things, enumerate them over and over in your mind, and thank Him for them.

Give thanks to the Lord daily for your mate. Instead of dwelling on the problems in your marriage, thank God for the blessings that you share together. Focus your attention on your spouse's strengths and thank God for them.

Some couples worry compulsively about a variety of issues facing them, putting undo pressure on the marital relationships. Keep in mind that the Bible says, *"Be anxious for nothing, but in everything by prayer and supplication with thanksgiving let your requests be made known to God"* (Philippians 4: 6).

Train yourself to thank God in spite of the often-chaotic circumstances swirling around your marriage.

Is gratitude to God a regular part of your prayer life? The Bible says it should be. When thanksgiving is a part of our prayers, we can expect the Lord to do great things.

Take a moment...

Is thanksgiving a regular part of your prayer life?

How often do you give thanks to the Lord for your mate?

Pray for Kings

Paul says we are to pray *"on behalf of **all** men"* (1 Timothy 2:1). We are to pray for unbelievers and Christians alike, for enemies and for friends – certainly our mates are included in this, as well.

Back in the first century, rabbis had developed the false belief that Jews were not to pray for Gentiles because they were only created to stoke the fires of hell. *[They had a very low opinion of the non-Jewish world.]* For Christians, however, there is no distinction or division in Christ Jesus; we pray for all men because God wants all men to be saved. Paul continues in verse 2: *"for kings and all who are in authority, so that we may lead a tranquil and quiet life in all godliness and dignity."*

Notice the all-encompassing, positive influence Christianity is to have: we are to pray for secular authorities. Too often, the Church has been accused of being against everything the world is for (and maybe rightfully so). The media portrays the Church as always demonstrating, protesting, and lobbying against the world, against government policies, and those holding political office. It is good to stand against the destructive elements in our society, but not to the extent that we appear to be *against* everything, and not *for* anything.

If as much effort would go into praying as people put into protesting, we would make some real headway for the Gospel. When we only lobby, protest, demonstrate, and condemn, we are sending the message that we think we can change society through the energy of the flesh. Surely God would ask, "Why don't you pray to Me, and let Me first change people's hearts?" We can work to change the veneer, but if the structure behind it is termite-eaten, it will soon collapse. Once you change the inner man, you solve the problems of the outer man.

It is true in marriage as well. You can coerce and badger your mate into doing "religious activities," but only prayer will change the heart.

This is the purpose of prayer: giving God permission to do what He already wants to do, but is waiting until He is asked before He steps in and does it. Proverbs 21:1 says that *"The king's heart is a stream of water in the hand of the Lord; He turns it wherever He will"* (NRSV). If God can turn the heart of a king, He can also turn the heart of your mate.

When we try to do in the energy of the flesh what only God can do by the power of His Spirit, we frustrate ourselves and our mates. God's response is, *" 'Not by might nor by power, but by My Spirit,' says the LORD of hosts"* (Zechariah 4:6).

Tertullian, one of the early church fathers, said: "We pray for all the emperors, that God may grant them long life, a secure government, a prosperous family, vigorous troops, a faithful senate, an obedient people; that the whole world may be in peace; and that God may grant, both to Caesar and to every man, the accomplishment of their just desires."[22]

A contemporary of Tertullian's, named Origen, was even more radical: "We pray for kings and rulers, that with their royal authority they may be found possessing a wise and prudent mind."[23] He insisted that our petitions would "vanquish all demons who stir up war ... and who disturb the peace."[24]

If we are to pray for government officials, who are at a distance from us, should we not pray for our own husbands and wives who are close by us? Should not a wife pray for the head of the family, her husband? And should not a husband pray that God would direct and lead his wife in the great responsibility she has in the home and with the children? If we do it for those that lead nations, should we not do it for our own who lead in the home?

Our son is a pastor who spent three terms as a legislator in the Hawaii State House of Representatives. He would keep us informed about upcoming legislation that could either help or hinder the moral climate here in Hawaii. It gave my wife and me an opportunity to join together in prayer *"for those in authority,"* as Paul exhorts.

This is a wonderful way for a couple to counteract the perception that Christians are far-removed from mainstream society. When we pray together about the issues facing our community, our nation, and the world, we become part of the solution, and not just a commentator on the problems.

Take a moment...

Are you praying for those in authority over you?

Have you ever let them know that you are praying for them?

Even secular people appreciate the average "Joe citizen" who loves God and prays for the country. I have found in my own experience that when non-believers hear that a Christian is praying for them, their families, their businesses, their health, etc., they are overjoyed and very grateful. They often feel that you as a Christian have a connection with "the Man upstairs" which they do not and it endears you to them.

A safe nation makes a secure society. That is a good reason why we should pray for government officials. Good rulers have the power to do much good for the nation and for the family, so pray for them to continue in that vein. Bad rulers can do much damage to a society, so we also need to pray that God would confuse and hinder their efforts for evil. The well-being of a nation and its families depends upon the character of its rulers; but whether they are good or bad, we have the power to influence God to influence them in a positive way. What a great ministry for every married couple.

We have a specific goal in mind when praying for our leaders: *"That we may lead a tranquil and quiet life in all godliness and dignity"* (1 Timothy 2:2). *Tranquility* carries the idea of bringing outward peace into society, a cessation of evil elements seeking access from the outside. A *quiet life* speaks of inward peace. Thus, when praying for rulers our goal is outward tranquility and inward peace, in all godliness. *Godliness* is our relationship toward God. And *dignity* represents our relationship toward one another.

When we have a right relationship with God and good fellowship with one another, our hearts dwell in a state of contentment and well-being. This is the ideal soil in which to cultivate a marriage that will truly live *happily ever after.*

LET'S DISCUSS
BATTLE-PLAN PRAYER...

1. Describe the results you have seen so far from the current "strategy of prayer" in your marriage.

   Do you have a goal in mind for your prayer life as a couple?

2. It has been said of Charles Spurgeon that he rarely prayed for more than five minutes...but he also rarely went without praying for more than five minutes.

   A healthy prayer life does not have to be difficult. What can a couple do to begin developing a strong prayer life?

   Give some ideas or personal examples.

3. James tells us, *"You do not have, because you do not ask God"* (James 4:2). What could be lacking in a marriage because of a lack of prayer?

4. Have you ever prayed about a situation in your marriage and found that God's answer was to change *your heart* more than *your circumstances*?

   Describe what happened.

   What did you learn from the situation?

LET'S APPLY WHAT WE'VE LEARNED...

1. What would you "entreat" (that is the prayer for the averting of evil)
    the Lord for in your marriage or family right now?

    Take time and do it.

2. Make a list of 10 things you can be thankful for in your marriage.

    1.

    2.

    3.

    4.

    5.

    6.

    7.

    8.

    9.

    10.

3. Give 5 examples of answered prayer in your marriage.

   1.

   2.

   3.

   4.

   5.

4. Are you praying for those in authority?

   When you pray, do you pray for the hearts of leaders to change, or only for the circumstances that affect you to change?

5. In your marriage, do you pray for your heart to change or only your mate's?

   Do you pray for a change of heart or only a change of circumstances?

I began this book with a pledge to get down in the marital trenches with you and help you learn how to battle the enemy for your marriage. I realize the difficulty in turning things around for the better in a relationship. You might feel your situation is an impossible task. You might say, "My mate is not interested in making the marriage work," or "My spouse is content with the 'status quo' while I am dying on the inside."

I learned a long time ago that you cannot have faith for another person's life; you can only have faith for your own life. There have been times in which I have tried injecting the faith that turned my marriage around into other couple's situation, but to no avail. No matter how encouraging or full of faith I might be for their relationship, I could not transfer my faith into their hearts and minds.

Some of you who read this book will work together with your husband or wife for change; others will have to work on things alone because your mate is not interested. I have been in both camps, and I know the challenges you face. But remember: You can only have faith for yourself (see Romans 14:22). Do not badger your mate in order to try to change them, pressuring them to be different than they are. Leave the changing to God. Remember that He is on your side, and "if God is for you, who can be against you?" (see Romans 8:31).

Although you cannot have faith for your partner, you certainly can pray for them. God wants to work in your marriage. Through prayer, we are simply asking Him to do what He already wants to do. And it is important to note that in the process of God working on the person you are praying for, He is also working on you.

No matter what the outcome, God has a wonderful plan for you. Seek first His kingdom and His righteousness, and He will add all things unto you and accomplish His plan for your life. Do not lose heart. God is able to do so much more than we could even think to ask Him. Even when things seem hopeless, remember that He is ready and willing – and is **already** at work in your life and marriage.

So my prayer for you, as you read and apply what you learn here about *Spiritual Warfare in Marriage*, is that the Lord would *"do abundantly above all you can think or ask, according to the riches of His glory in Christ Jesus"* (Ephesians 3: 16,20). Amen.

- *Married And How To Stay That Way*
  by Steve Carr
  ACW Press, ISBN-13: 978-0965674935

- *The Christian Family*
  by Larry Christenson
  Bethany House, ISBN-13: 978-0871231147

- *Solomon On Sex*
  by Joseph Dillow
  Thomas Nelson Inc, ISBN-13: 978-0840758132

- *The Greatest Thing In The World*
  by Henry Drummond
  Book Jungle, ISBN-13: 978-1604244205

- *The Effective Father*
  by Gordon MacDonald
  Highland Books, ISBN-13: 978-0946616633

- *The Myth Of The Greener Grass*
  by J. Allan Petersen
  Tyndale House Publishers, ISBN-13: 978-0842346511

- *Christian Family Relationships*
  by Chuck Smith, ID: 0936728043

- *Strike The Original Match*
  by Chuck Swindoll
  Alpha, ISBN-13: 978-1872059396

- *How To Pray*
  by R. A. Torrey
  University of Michigan Library, ASIN: B002KAOOV4

- *The Kneeling Christian*
  Unknown Author
  CreateSpace, ISBN-13: 978-1448656752

- *Love Life For Every Married Couple*
  by Dr. Ed Wheat
  Zondervan, ISBN-13: 978-0310214861

- *Do Yourself A Favor, Love Your Wife*
  by H. Page Williams
  Bridge-Logos, ISBN-13: 978-0882702049

FOOTNOTES

CHAPTER ONE

[1] Paul Harvey, Jr. Adapted from the original story found in *More of Paul Harvey's the Rest of the Story*. Bantam Books, a division of Random House, Inc., New York, NY, 1984.

[2] Provisional Number of Marriages and Divorces: Each Division and State, December 1998–99, and Cumulative Figures, 1997–99. National Vital Statistics Report; Volume 48, No. 19. <http://www.cdc.gov/nchs/data/nvsr/nvsr48/48_19_3.pdf> (October 6, 2003).

[3] William Glasser. *Reality Therapy: A New Approach to Psychiatry*. HarperCollins Publishers, New York, NY, December 1975.

[4] David Popenoe. "The Top Ten Myths of Divorce." The National Marriage Project, the State University of New Jersey, Rutgers, <http://marriage.rutgers.edu/Publications/pubtoptenmyths.htm #back1> (August 29, 2003).

[5] *Divorce Magazine.com*. "U.S. Divorce Statistics." <http://www.divorcemag.com/statistics/statsUS.shtml> (August 29, 2003).

[6] Paul Mauchline. "Love on the Other Side of the Fence." <http://enotalone.com/article/1059.html> (August 29, 2003).

[7] Nadia Lerner. "Cyber cheats" from *The Stamford Advocate*, reprinted in AugustaChronicle.com, July 29, 1999 <http://www.augustachronicle.com/stories/072999/tec_UX9461-0.000.shtml> (August 29, 2003).

[8] Ibid.

[9] Ibid.

[10] Ibid.

[11] Ibid.

Chapter Four

12 *U.S. News & World Report*, February 21, 1994, p. 67

13 Albert Mehrabian. *Nonverbal Communication*. Aldine-Atherton, Chicago, Illinois, 1972.

Chapter Five

14 This story was told at a Calvary Chapel pastor's conference.

15 Attributed to Saint Ivo (Yves) of Chartres.

Chapter Six

16 Matthew Henry. (from *Matthew Henry's Commentary on the Whole Bible*: New Modern Edition, Electronic Database. Copyright © 1991 by Hendrickson Publishers, Inc.) [commenting on 1 Timothy 2:1.] All rights reserved.

17 Paraphrased from *The Complete Word Study New Testament* edited by Spiros Zodhiates, Th.D.

18 Ibid.

19 Taken in part from Jay Barnes. *North Carolina's Hurricane History*. UNC Press, June 1998. Also taken in part from a brochure on "The Church Moved by the Hand of God." <http://homepages.rootsweb.com/~jmack/photos/providen.htm> (September 3, 2003).

20 Paraphrased from *The Complete Word Study New Testament* edited by Spiros Zodhiates, Th.D.

21 Biblesoft's *New Exhaustive Strong's Numbers and Concordance with Expanded Greek-Hebrew Dictionary*. Copyright ©1994 Biblesoft and International Bible Translators, Inc. All rights reserved.

22 Adam Clarke. (from *Adam Clarke's Commentary*, Electronic Database. Copyright © 1996 by Biblesoft.) [Commenting on 1 Timothy 2:2.] All rights reserved.

23 Ibid.

24 From Origen's *Contra Celsus*, Book VIII, Chapter LXXIII—translated from Volume 4 of *The Ante-Nicene Fathers*, Public Domain. <http://www.ccel.org/fathers2/ANF-04/anf04-63.htm#P11216_3045285> (September 3, 2003).

ABOUT THE AUTHOR

Bill Stonebraker was born in Minnesota but raised in Southern California. Like many people today, he grew up in an unstable home, his mother divorcing and re-marrying several times. He knew what it was like to be without the positive influence of a consistent mother and father in his life.

Although he did have an experience with Jesus at an young age, Bill really came to faith in Christ in the early '70s, then living in Hawaii as a surfboard manufacturer with a troubled marriage. A Bible study began in his home on Oahu's North Shore among the local surfing community, and eventually birthed the *North Shore Christian Fellowship* – still a thriving congregation in Haleiwa, Hawaii.

In the early '80s, Bill turned *NSCF* over to his associate pastor and began *Calvary Chapel of Honolulu*, where he currently pastors. His radio, television and internet teaching ministry is called *"As We Gather."* Bill's dedication to the principle of "simply teaching the Bible simply" has seen him invited to speak all over the world, including conferences in Australia, Japan, Ethiopia, Uganda, Israel, Fiji, South Africa, and Puerto Rico.

Following years of renting various venues for its weekly services, in 2004 *Calvary Chapel of Honolulu* opened a Church-School campus on six acres in central Oahu. Along with its main church sanctuary, the property also includes *The Chapel Store* Christian bookstore, the studios of *KLHT Radio* (1040 AM), *Calvary Chapel Christian Preschool*, and *Calvary Chapel Christian School*, covering Kindergarten through High School.

God healed Bill and Danita Stonebraker's marriage and has used them over the years to counsel countless other couples struggling in their relationships. This book, *Spiritual Warfare in Marriage*, is based on teachings originally given live by Bill and Danita at a marriage conference in Honolulu, Hawaii.

For more information on audio or video teachings by Bill Stonebraker, or to learn more about Calvary Chapel of Honolulu, please visit our website at:

www.calvarychapelofhonolulu.com

You can also contact us at:

Calvary Chapel of Honolulu
98-1016 Komo Mai Drive
Aiea, Hawaii 96701

Notes